CliffsNotes™

To Kill a Mockingbird

By Tamara Castleman

IN THIS BOOK

- Learn about the Life and Background of the Author
- Preview an Introduction to the Novel
- Explore themes, character development, and recurring images in the Critical Commentaries
- Examine in-depth Character Analyses
- Acquire an understanding of the novel with Critical Essays
- Reinforce what you learn with CliffsNotes Review
- Find additional information to further your study in CliffsNotes Resource Center and online at www.cliffsnotes.com

WILEY

Wiley Publishing, Inc.

About the Author

Tamara Castleman, a graduate of Indiana University, Bloomington, Indiana, is a writer, editor, and literacy advocate.

Publisher's Acknowledgments

Editorial

Project Editor: Mary Goodwin

Acquisitions Editor: Greg Tubach

Editorial Administrator: Michelle Hacker

Glossary Editors: The editors and staff of Webster's New World Dictionaries

Composition

Indexer: York Production Services, Inc.

Proofreader: York Production Services, Inc.

Wiley Indianapolis Composition Services

CliffsNotes™ *To Kill a Mockingbird*

Published by:
Wiley Publishing, Inc.
111 River Street
Hoboken, NJ 07030
www.wiley.com

Copyright © 2000 Wiley Publishing, Inc., New York, New York
ISBN: 978-0-7645-8600-2
Printed in the United States of America
15 14 13
1O/TQ/QW/QW/IN
Published by Wiley Publishing, Inc., Hoboken, NJ
Published simultaneously in Canada

Library of Congress Cataloging-in-Publication Data
Castleman, Tamara Shelline, 1965-
    CliffsNotes To Kill a Mockingbird / Tamara
Shelline Castleman.
        p.   cm.
    Includes index.
    ISBN 978-0-7645-8600-2 (alk. paper)
    1. Lee, Harper. To Kill a Mockingbird--
Examinations--Study guides. I. Title: To Kill a
Mockingbird. II. Title
PS3562.E353 T6332 2000
811'.54--dc21   00–038864
                                                        CIP

Table of Contents

How to Use This Book

This CliffsNotes study guide on Harper Lee's *To Kill a Mockingbird* sup-plements the original literary work, giving you background information about the author, an introduction to the work, a graphical character map, critical commentaries, expanded glossaries, and a comprehensive index, all for you to use as an educational tool that will allow you to better understand *To Kill a Mockingbird*. This study guide was written with the assumption that you have read *To Kill a Mockingbird*. Reading a literary work doesn't mean that you immediately grasp the major themes and devices used by the author; this study guide will help supplement your reading to be sure you get all you can from Harper Lee's *To Kill a Mockingbird*. CliffsNotes Review tests your comprehension of the original text and reinforces learning with questions and answers, practice projects, and more. For further information on Harper Lee and *To Kill a Mockingbird*, check out the CliffsNotes Resource Center.

CliffsNotes provides the following icons to highlight essential elements of particular interest:

Reveals the underlying themes in the work.

Helps you to more easily relate to or discover the depth of a character.

Uncovers elements such as setting, atmosphere, mystery, passion, violence, irony, symbolism, tragedy, foreshadowing, and satire.

Enables you to appreciate the nuances of words and phrases.

Don't Miss Our Web Site

Discover classic literature as well as modern-day treasures by visiting the CliffsNotes Web site at www.cliffsnotes.com. You can obtain a quick download of a CliffsNotes title, purchase a title in print form, browse our catalog, or view online samples.

LIFE AND BACKGROUND OF THE AUTHOR

The following abbreviated biography of Harper Lee is provided so that you might become more familiar with her life and the historical times that possibly influenced her writing. Read this Life and Background of the Author section and recall it when reading Lee's *To Kill a Mockingbird*, thinking of any thematic relationship between Lee's novel and her life.

The youngest daughter of Amasa Coleman Lee and Frances Cunningham Finch Lee, Nelle Harper Lee was born in Monroeville, Alabama (a small town in Monroe County between Montgomery and Mobile) on April 28, 1926. Lee was raised with two sisters, Alice and Louise, and a brother, Edwin Coleman Lee. Both her sisters are still living, but her brother died of a sudden cerebral hemorrhage in 1951.

Amasa Lee grew up in Florida and came to Monroe County in the early 1900s. He worked as a bookkeeper until 1915, when he passed the bar and began practicing law. Mr. Lee also served on the Alabama State Legislature from 1926 to 1938, and as editor of *The Monroe Journal* from 1929 to 1947.

Frances Finch was from a Virginia family who settled in Monroe County, Alabama, and founded the town of Finchburg. Miss Finch met Mr. Lee while he was working at the Flat Creek Mill Company in Finchburg; they married in 1912. The couple lived briefly in Florida, returning to live in Monroe County in 1913.

By all accounts, Harper Lee is friendly and gregarious with those she knows, but has always been an extremely private person, disclosing little about her life to the public. Consequently, most of the information available about Lee's childhood comes from friends and is largely anecdotal. Because the character of Scout is somewhat autobiographical, readers gain their best access to Lee's childhood—or at least the flavor of her childhood—within the pages of *To Kill a Mockingbird.*

In 1944, at the age of 18, Harper Lee enrolled in Huntingdon College in Montgomery, Alabama. From 1945 to 1949 she studied law at the University of Alabama. She transferred to Oxford University in England as an exchange student for a year, but six months before completing her studies, Lee decided to go to New York to be a writer.

While pursuing the career that would ultimately produce *To Kill a Mockingbird*, Lee worked briefly in the early 1950s as a reservations clerk for Eastern Airlines and BOAC (British Overseas Airways Corp.) in New York City. In 1957, she submitted a manuscript to the J. B. Lippincott Company, who felt that her attempt at a novel was actually more of a series of strung-together short stories. The publisher recommended a rewrite, so Lee spent the next two-and-a-half years working on the manuscript. Her efforts paid off, and *To Kill a Mockingbird*, her first and only novel, was published in 1960.

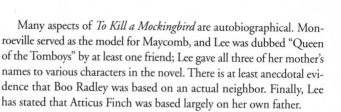

Many aspects of *To Kill a Mockingbird* are autobiographical. Monroeville served as the model for Maycomb, and Lee was dubbed "Queen of the Tomboys" by at least one friend; Lee gave all three of her mother's names to various characters in the novel. There is at least anecdotal evidence that Boo Radley was based on an actual neighbor. Finally, Lee has stated that Atticus Finch was based largely on her own father.

To Kill a Mockingbird was awarded the Pulitzer Prize in 1961, and was made into a major motion picture starring Gregory Peck in 1962. Lee was so impressed with Peck's portrayal of Atticus Finch that she gave him her father's pocket watch at the end of the movie's filming.

In the early 1960s, shortly after publication of *To Kill a Mockingbird*, Harper Lee accompanied her childhood friend Truman Capote— the basis for the Dill Harris character— to Holcomb, Kansas, and served as a research assistant for Capote's 1966 novel, *In Cold Blood*.

Lee also published three articles in the '60s: "Love—In Other Words" in *Vogue* (1961), "Christmas to Me" in *McCalls* (1961), and "When Children Discover America" in *McCalls* (1965). President Lyndon Johnson named Lee to the National Council of Arts in 1966. She has received several honorary doctorates, including one from the University of Alabama and another from Spring Hill College in Mobile, Alabama. She attended both ceremonies, but spoke at neither and gave no interviews.

In 1998, the Harper Lee Award for a Distinguished Alabama Writer was unveiled by the executive committee of the Alabama Writers' Forum. This award recognizes an accomplished writer who was born in the state or who lived in Alabama during his or her formative years.

Never married, Lee continues to divide her time between New York and Monroeville, where she lives with her sister Alice. Known for her wit and charm, Lee has granted only a handful of interviews since *To Kill a Mockingbird's* publication. Her family and friends remain protective of her privacy.

Many wonder why a writer of such talent would choose to write only one novel. When Lee's cousin, Richard Williams, posed that question to the author, her answer was "When you have a hit like that, you can't go anywhere but down."

INTRODUCTION TO THE NOVEL

The following Introduction section is provided solely as an educational tool and is not meant to replace the experience of your reading the novel. Read the Introduction and A Brief Synopsis to enhance your understanding of the novel and to prepare yourself for the critical thinking that should take place whenever you read any work of fiction or nonfiction. Keep the List of Characters and Character Map at hand so that as you read the original literary work, if you encounter a character about whom you're uncertain, you can refer to the List of Characters and Character Map to refresh your memory.

Introduction

When Harper Lee wrote *To Kill a Mockingbird*, her home state of Alabama was a hotbed of Civil Rights activity. Throughout the South, blacks and whites were segregated. African-Americans used different drinking fountains, entrances, and restroom facilities. They also had to sit on the back of public buses and were expected to move if a white person wanted a seat. In 1955, Rosa Parks refused to give up her seat on a Montgomery, Alabama bus. Her momentous decision sparked a yearlong bus boycott, giving new life to the Civil Rights movement and propelling Martin Luther King, Jr. to national prominence. Civil Rights issues were heating up across the nation, too, and so the subject of *To Kill a Mockingbird* was quite timely upon its publication.

Lee, however, chose to set her story in the Great Depression of the 1930s. She may have had many reasons for placing the story in that time. Scout, the story's protagonist and narrator, is a semi-autobiographical character, and Lee was roughly the same age as Scout in the 1930s. Also, writers often choose to place a story about a current issue in the past or in the future to give readers an objective place from which to ponder the issue. Most likely, though, Lee chose the 1930s because Civil Rights issues didn't just begin in the late 1950s. The Civil Rights movement had a long history of making "baby-step[s]," as one character in the story would say, before it gelled into a cohesive effort. Racial relations were tense during the Depression because African-Americans and Caucasians were competing for the same jobs in an environment where few jobs were available. Whites, particularly in the South, began to demand that they be given the jobs that were going to blacks. Furthermore, many whites actually fell prey to the mentality that blacks were stealing jobs from them, making a tense situation worse.

Beyond the issues of racial relations and the injustices that minority groups suffered during this time, Lee's novel is also a coming-of-age story, or *Bildungsroman*. In this type of story, the central character moves from a state of innocence to one of maturity as the result of suffering and surviving various misadventures. In *To Kill a Mockingbird*, Scout Finch is that central character, and one of her biggest concerns throughout the book is coming to terms with the expectations her society has for women. In the 1930s, women in the South were pressured to conform to a widely held ideal of "Southern womanhood." Women were treated as delicate, fragile creatures, and they were expected to act in accordance with that treatment. Scout is anything but delicate and fragile, and a good deal of the story focuses on her attempts to fit into a world that expects tomboys to wear frilly dresses and maintain a dainty disposition.

The characters grapple with other themes and questions as well: bravery and cowardice; tolerance; compassion; conscience; reason; societal expectations; and, prejudice at all levels. That Lee fully develops such a broad range of themes in a relatively short novel is a testimony to her talent and the story's brilliance.

A Brief Synopsis

To Kill a Mockingbird is primarily a novel about growing up under extraordinary circumstances in the 1930s in the Southern United States. The story covers a span of three years, during which the main characters undergo significant changes. Scout Finch lives with her brother Jem and their father Atticus in the fictitious town of Maycomb, Alabama. Maycomb is a small, close-knit town, and every family has its social station depending on where they live, who their parents are, and how long their ancestors have lived in Maycomb.

A widower, Atticus raises his children by himself, with the help of kindly neighbors and a black housekeeper named Calpurnia. Scout and Jem almost instinctively understand the complexities and machinations of their neighborhood and town. The only neighbor who puzzles them is the mysterious Arthur Radley, nicknamed Boo, who never comes outside. When Dill, another neighbor's nephew, starts spending summers in Maycomb, the three children begin an obsessive—and sometimes perilous—quest to lure Boo outside.

Scout is a tomboy who prefers the company of boys and generally solves her differences with her fists. She tries to make sense of a world that demands that she act like a lady, a brother who criticizes her for acting like a girl, and a father who accepts her just as she is. Scout hates school, gaining her most valuable education on her own street and from her father.

Not quite midway through the story, Scout and Jem discover that their father is going to represent a black man named Tom Robinson, who is accused of raping and beating a white woman. Suddenly, Scout and Jem have to tolerate a barrage of racial slurs and insults because of Atticus' role in the trial. During this time, Scout has a very difficult time restraining from physically fighting with other children, a tendency that gets her in trouble with her Aunt Alexandra and Uncle Jack. Even Jem, the older and more levelheaded of the two, loses his temper a time or two. After responding to a neighbor's (Mrs. Dubose) verbal attack by destroying her plants, Jem is sentenced to read to her every day after school for one month. Ultimately, Scout and Jem learn a powerful lesson about bravery from this woman. As the trial draws nearer, Aunt Alexandra comes to live with them under the guise of providing a feminine influence for Scout.

During the novel's last summer, Tom is tried and convicted even though Atticus proves that Tom could not have possibly committed the crime of which he is accused. In the process of presenting Tom's case, Atticus inadvertently insults and offends Bob Ewell, a nasty, lazy drunkard whose daughter is Tom's accuser. In spite of Tom's conviction, Ewell vows revenge on Atticus and the judge for besmirching his already tarnished name. All three children are bewildered by the jury's decision to convict; Atticus tries to explain why the jury's decision was in many ways a foregone conclusion.

Shortly after the trial, Scout attends one of her aunt's Missionary Society meetings. Atticus interrupts the meeting to report that Tom Robinson had been killed in an escape attempt. Scout learns valuable lessons about achieving the ideal of womanhood and carrying on in the face of adversity that day.

Things slowly return to normal in Maycomb, and Scout and Jem realize that Boo Radley is no longer an all-consuming curiosity. The story appears to be winding down, but then Bob Ewell starts making good on his threats of revenge. Scout is in the Halloween pageant at school, playing the part of a ham. With Atticus and Aunt Alexandra both too tired to attend, Jem agrees to take Scout to the school. After embarrassing herself on-stage, Scout elects to leave her ham costume on for the walk home with Jem.

On the way home, the children hear odd noises, but convince themselves that the noises are coming from another friend who scared them on their way to school that evening. Suddenly, a scuffle occurs. Scout really can't see outside of her costume, but she hears Jem being pushed away, and she feels powerful arms squeezing her costume's chicken wire against her skin. During this attack, Jem badly breaks his arm. Scout gets just enough of a glimpse out of her costume to see a stranger carrying Jem back to their house.

The sheriff arrives at the Finch house to announce that Bob Ewell has been found dead under the tree where the children were attacked, having fallen on his own knife. By this time, Scout realizes that the stranger is none other than Boo Radley, and that Boo is actually responsible for killing Ewell, thus saving her and Jem's lives. In spite of Atticus' insistence to the contrary, the sheriff refuses to press charges against Boo. Scout agrees with this decision and explains her understanding to her father. Boo sees Jem one more time and then asks Scout to take him home, but rather than escort him home as though he were a child, she has Boo escort her to his house as a gentleman would.

With Boo safely home, Scout returns to Jem's room where Atticus is waiting. He reads her to sleep and then waits by Jem's bedside for his son to wake up.

List of Characters

Scout (Jean Louise Finch) Narrator of the story. The story takes place from the time Scout is aged 6 to 9, but she tells the story as an adult. Scout is a tomboy who would rather solve problems with her fists than with her head. Throughout the course of the book, Scout comes to a new understanding of human nature, societal expectations, and her own place in the world.

Atticus Finch Maycomb attorney and state legislative representative who is assigned to represent Tom Robinson. A widower, Atticus is a single parent to two children: Jem and Scout.

Jem (Jeremy Atticus Finch) Scout's older brother who ages from 10 to 13 during the story. He is Scout's protector and one of her best friends. As part of reaching young adulthood, Jem deals with many difficult issues throughout the story.

Aunt Alexandra Atticus' sister. Aunt Alexandra lives at Finch's Landing, the Finch family homestead, but she moves in with Atticus and the children during Tom Robinson's trial. She is very concerned that Scout have a feminine influence to emulate.

Francis Hancock Aunt Alexandra's grandson. He taunts Scout about Atticus, getting her in trouble.

Uncle Jack Finch Atticus and Aunt Alexandra's bachelor brother who comes to visit every Christmas. He is a doctor who, like Atticus, was schooled at home.

Calpurnia The Finch's Negro housekeeper. She grew up at Finch's Landing and moved with Atticus to Maycomb. She is the closest thing to a mother that Scout and Jem have. One of the few Negroes in town who can read and write, she teaches Scout to write.

Zeebo The town garbage collector who is also Calpurnia's son. He's one of four people who can read at the First Purchase African M.E. Church.

Boo Radley (Mr. Arthur Radley) The mysterious neighbor who piques the children's interest. They've never seen him and make a game of trying to get him to come outside.

Nathan Radley Boo Radley's brother who comes back to live with the family when Mr. Radley dies.

Mr. and Mrs. Radley Boo and Nathan Radley's parents.

Dill (Charles Baker Harris) Jem and Scout's neighborhood friend. Living in Meridian, Mississippi, Dill spends every summer with his aunt, Miss Rachel Haverford.

Miss Rachel Haverford Dill's aunt who lives next door to the Finches.

Miss Maudie Atkinson One of Maycomb's most open-minded citizens, Miss Maudie lives across the street from Jem and Scout. An avid gardener, she often spends time talking with the children—especially Scout—helping them to better understand Atticus and their community.

Miss Stephanie Crawford The neighborhood gossip.

Mrs. Henry Lafayette Dubose A cantankerous, vile, elderly woman who teaches Jem and Scout a great lesson in bravery.

Mrs. Grace Merriweather A devout Methodist, Mrs. Merriweather writes the Halloween pageant.

Mrs. Gertrude Farrow The "second most devout lady in Maycomb" belongs to the local Missionary Society.

Tom Robinson The black man who is accused of raping and beating Mayella Ewell.

Helen Robinson Tom Robinson's wife.

Link Deas Tom and Helen Robinson's employer. He makes sure that Helen can pass safely by the Ewell's after Tom is arrested.

Bob Ewell The Ewell patriarch, Bob Ewell spends his welfare checks on alcohol. He claims to have witnessed Tom attacking Mayella.

Mayella Violet Ewell Tom's 19-year-old accuser.

Burris Ewell One of Bob Ewell's children. He attends school only one day a year.

Reverend Skyes The pastor at First Purchase African M.E. Church. He helps Jem and Scout understand Tom's trial and finds seats for them in the "colored balcony."

Judge John Taylor The judge at Tom's trial. He appoints Atticus to represent Tom.

Mr. Horace Gilmer The state attorney representing the Ewells.

Sheriff Heck Tate Maycomb's sheriff who accompanies Atticus to kill the mad dog and who delivers the news about Bob Ewell.

Mr. Braxton Bragg Underwood The owner, editor, and printer of *The Maycomb Tribune*. Although he openly dislikes blacks, he defends Tom's right to a fair trial.

Dolphus Raymond Father to several biracial children, Mr. Raymond lives on the outskirts of town. When he comes into Maycomb, he pretends to be drunk.

Walter Cunningham, Sr. One of the men who comes to lynch Tom Robinson, he's also one of Atticus' clients. After speaking with Scout, he calls off the mob.

Walter Cunningham, Jr. One of Scout's classmates. Jem invites him to have lunch with them after Scout accosts Walter on the playground.

Miss Caroline Fisher New to teaching and to Maycomb and its ways, Miss Caroline is Scout's first grade teacher.

Cecil Jacobs A schoolmate of the Finch children, he scares Jem and Scout on the way to the Halloween pageant.

Little Chuck Little One of Scout's classmates who stands up to Burris Ewell in defense of Miss Caroline.

Miss Gates Scout's second grade teacher.

Lula A parishioner at First Purchase African M.E. Church who is upset when Scout and Jem attend services there.

Eula May The local telephone operator.

Mr. Avery A boarder at the house across from Mrs. Dubose's.

Character Map

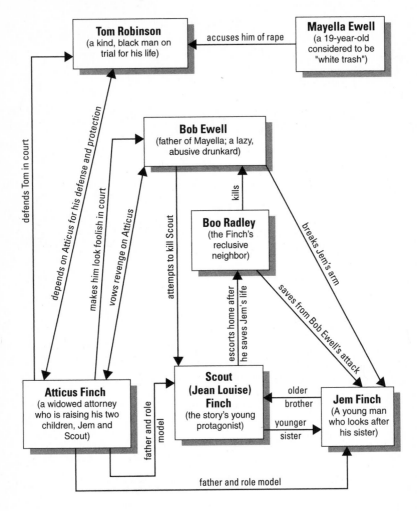

Tom Robinson (a kind, black man on trial for his life)

Mayella Ewell (a 19-year-old considered to be "white trash")

accuses him of rape

Bob Ewell (father of Mayella; a lazy, abusive drunkard)

Boo Radley (the Finch's reclusive neighbor)

kills

breaks Jem's arm

defends Tom in court

depends on Atticus for his defense and protection

makes him look foolish in court

vows revenge on Atticus

attempts to kill Scout

escorts home after he saves Jem's life

saves from Bob Ewell's attack

Atticus Finch (a widowed attorney who is raising his two children, Jem and Scout)

Scout (Jean Louise) Finch (the story's young protagonist)

Jem Finch (A young man who looks after his sister)

older brother

younger sister

father and role model

father and role model

CRITICAL COMMENTARIES

The sections that follow provide great tools for supplementing your reading of *To Kill a Mockingbird*. First, in order to enhance your understanding of and enjoyment from reading, we provide quick summaries in case you have difficulty when you read the original literary work. Each summary is followed by commentary: literary devices, character analyses, themes, and so on. Keep in mind that the interpretations here are solely those of the author of this study guide and are used to jumpstart your thinking about the work. No single interpretation of a complex work like *To Kill a Mockingbird* is infallible or exhaustive, and you'll likely find that you interpret portions of the work differently from the author of this study guide. Read the original work and determine your own interpretations, referring to these Notes for supplemental meanings only.

Epigraph

Lee begins *To Kill a Mockingbird* with an epigraph (a brief quotation placed at the beginning of a book or chapter) by Charles Lamb: *"Lawyers, I suppose, were children once."* That she chose this epigraph is interesting on several levels.

A good part of this story's brilliance lies in the fact that it's told from a child's point of view. Through Scout's eyes, Lee is able to present the story objectively. By having an innocent little girl make racial remarks and regard people of color in a way consistent with the community, Lee provides an objective view of the situation. As a child, Scout can make observations that an adult would avoid or sugarcoat. Readers, too, are likely to be forgiving of a child's perception, whereas they would find an adult who makes these remarks offensive.

Much of Harper Lee is in the character of Scout. Lee's father was an attorney, as is Scout's. Importantly, Lee herself studied law. Because Scout's personality is loosely autobiographical, the epigraph makes sense. Lee proves through the telling of the story that she was also once a child.

Also significant in understanding the epigraph is Atticus' answer to Jem's question of how a jury could convict Tom Robinson when he's obviously innocent: "'They've done it before and they did it tonight and they'll do it again and when they do it—it seems that only children weep.'" At various points in the story, Jem expresses his desire to become a lawyer, following in his father's footsteps. The lessons he learns during the course of the story will ultimately shape not only the kind of lawyer he will be, but also the kind of man he will become. Readers see this future lawyer as a child first.

Part One
Chapter 1

Summary

Scout, the narrator, remembers the summer that her brother Jem broke his arm, and she looks back over the years to recall the incidents that led to that climactic event. Scout provides a brief introduction to the town of Maycomb, Alabama and its inhabitants, including her widowed father Atticus Finch, attorney and state legislator; Calpurnia, their "Negro" cook and housekeeper; and various neighbors.

The story starts with the first summer that Scout and Jem meet Dill, a little boy from Meridian, Mississippi who spends the summers with his aunt, the Finch's next-door neighbor Miss Rachel Haverford.

From the children's point of view, their most compelling neighbor is Boo Radley, a recluse whom none of them has ever seen. Dill's fascination, in particular, leads to all sorts of games and plans to try and get Boo to come outside. Their attempts culminate in a dare to Jem, which he grudgingly takes. Jem runs into the Radley's yard and touches the outside of the house.

Commentary

This chapter sets the tone and basis for everything else that happens in the novel. Scout depicts her world as a place of absolutes. This strong foundation provides an important starting point for the story. Subsequent situations and circumstances chip away at all that the children know to be true as maturity confronts them. This maturity is foreshadowed by Jem's broken arm and the fact that the story is told in retrospect.

Literary Device

Novels that deal with the formation of a maturing character are called *Bildungsromans* or *coming-of-age stories*. Scout as narrator is key to the novel's success. The reader has the advantage of a storyteller who can look back at a situation and see herself exactly as she was. Scout tells the story from an adult point-of-view but with a child's eye and voice, which gives the story a good deal of humor and wit. Scout's distance from the story also gives her some objectivity, although she admits that even in her objectivity, some events are questionable: "I maintain that the Ewell's started it all, but Jem . . . said it started long before that."

The sense of place established in this chapter is integral to the rest of the story. Through Scout, Lee gives the reader a feel for the small southern town of Maycomb, Alabama, which is loosely based on Lee's hometown of Monroeville, Alabama. In this town, the rules of society are clearly set. One's social survival depends on how well he or she follows the rules. Scout, Jem, and Dill come to question these conventions as the story progresses.

Where a person comes from—his ancestry—is important, and like many small towns, Maycomb's citizens are suspicious of outsiders. Dill is a crucial character in the story because he is both an insider and an outsider. He hails from a different state, but because he is a child and because "His family was from Maycomb originally," he is accepted readily. Throughout the story, Dill acts as an observant conscience for the town. The first example of Dill as conscience comes when he and Jem disagree about the method for making a turtle come out of its shell.

Theme

A hefty portion of the story focuses on prejudice and the relationships between African Americans and whites in the southern United States in general, and Maycomb, specifically. This chapter makes clear that Maycomb has very different rules for blacks and whites in the town, as evidenced by the children's surprise when Calpurnia speaks ill of Boo Radley's father because "Calpurnia rarely commented on the ways of white people."

Superstition is brought to light in the children's perception of Boo Radley. Much like a mystery novel, the first chapter gives readers the idea that things may not be what they seem on the surface, as when Scout's father, Atticus, says "there were other ways of making people into ghosts."

Scout gives readers their first insights into Atticus Finch in this chapter, as well. A patient and loving, if somewhat unusual, father, Atticus acts as the voice of reason for his children, and later the entire town. The fact that he has a "profound distaste for criminal law" foreshadows the emotions he has surrounding Tom Robinson's trial later in the story.

Another major theme in the novel that is introduced in this chapter is that of defining bravery. For the children at this point in the story, bravery means nothing more than accepting a dare to touch the Radley house.

Glossary

(Here and in the following chapters, difficult words and phrases, as well as allusions and historical references, are explained.)

"swept yard" in some areas of the South, a swept yard was a sign of a well-kept home. A swept yard was typically kept neat and clean using straw sagebrush brooms.

flivver [Old Slang] a small, cheap automobile, esp. an old one.

beadle [Obs.] a messenger of a law court.

neighborhood scold a person, esp. a woman, who habitually uses abusive language.

Cannas any of a genus *(Canna)* of broad-leaved tropical plants, often grown for ornament because of the striking foliage and brilliant flowers.

The Gray Ghost one in a series of pulp fiction novels written in 1926 by Robert Schulkers. These humorous mystery stories were narrated by Seckatary Hawkins, the "seckatary" of a boy's club.

Tom Swift boys' pulp fiction serial featuring famed, fictitious inventor and adventurer, Tom Swift.

Chapters 2 and 3

Summary

Dill goes back to Mississippi for the school year, and Scout turns her attention to starting first grade—something she's been waiting for all her life. However, Scout's first day at school is not at all the glorious experience she'd been expecting from the winters she spent "looking over at the schoolyard, spying on multitudes of children through a two-power telescope . . . learning their games, . . . secretly sharing their misfortunes and minor victories."

Scout's teacher, Miss Caroline Fisher, is new to teaching, new to Maycomb, and mortified that Scout already knows how to read and write. When Miss Caroline offers to lend Walter Cunningham lunch money, Scout is punished for taking it upon herself to explain Miss Caroline's faux pas to her. (Walter refuses to take the money because his family is too poor to pay it back.)

Scout catches Walter on the playground, and starts to pummel him in retaliation for her embarrassment, but Jem stops her and then further surprises her by inviting Walter to have lunch with them. Scout is then punished by Calpurnia for criticizing Walter's table manners. Back at school, Miss Caroline has a confrontation with Burris Ewell about his "cooties" and the fact that he only attends school on the first day of the year.

That evening, Scout tells Atticus about her day, hoping that she won't have to go back to school—after all, Burris Ewell doesn't. Atticus explains why the Ewells get special consideration and then tells Scout, "'You never really understand a person . . . until you climb into his skin and walk around in it.'" These words stick with Scout, and she will try with varying degrees of success to follow Atticus' advice throughout the course of the story.

Commentary

In these two chapters, Lee uses Scout to help the reader gain a better understanding of the Maycomb community and how it functions. Meeting Scout's classmates paves the way for meeting their adult family members later in the book. The children introduced in these chapters are a microcosm of their families. For instance, Walter Cunningham, like his father, is polite, self-effacing, and unwilling to accept charity. The reader also learns that the Ewells are an unsavory family. Burris Ewell displays the same sort of character traits that make his father, Bob Ewell, so dislikable.

Scout considers her first day of school to be a dismal failure, and compared to what she was hoping for, it is. However, she learns a great deal about people in and out of the classroom. In one day's time, Scout learns several important lessons, but most importantly, she gets her first inkling that things are not always what they seem.

Scout is different from other children. Miss Caroline's harsh reaction to the fact that Scout already knows how to read and write takes the little girl by surprise. Doesn't everyone already know how to read and write? Scout laments, "I never deliberately learned to read, but somehow had been wallowing illicitly in the daily papers"—one of many humorous observations that Lee sprinkles through these two chapters and throughout the book. Even more astounding to Scout is the fact that Miss Caroline expects her to stop reading and writing at home now that she's in school.

Style & Language

Scout is all the more confused because her father is not like the authority figures she meets at school. Atticus is not a typical parent. Lee does an expert job of getting this message across to readers simply by having the children call Atticus by his first name. He treats his children as individuals and speaks to them in an adult-like manner. Scout accepts this behavior as normal noting, "Jem and I were accustomed to our father's last-will-and-testament diction, and we were at all times free to interrupt Atticus for a translation when it was beyond our understanding." Perhaps if Miss Caroline had reasoned with Scout, the day would not have been so devastating for either of them.

Other people don't understand "Maycomb's ways." Harper Lee again emphasizes that outsiders are viewed with suspicion. When Miss Caroline announces her county of origin, "The class murmured apprehensively, should she prove to harbor her share of the peculiarities indigenous to that region."

When Scout tries to explain Walter Cunningham's predicament to Miss Caroline by simply saying, "'he's a Cunningham,'" she remarks to readers "I thought I had made things sufficiently clear. It was clear enough to the rest of us." The children don't expect Miss Caroline to understand the intricacies of their town, but they're forced to expand their worldview when they realize that "a Cunningham is a Cunningham" is not explanation enough for a Maycomb newcomer.

Ironically, Scout soon learns that she doesn't understand as much about "Maycomb's ways" as she thinks. When Scout uses Burris Ewell's lack of regular school attendance as a good reason that she shouldn't have to go to school either, Atticus explains that "In certain circumstances, the common folk judiciously allowed them certain privileges by the simple method of becoming blind to some of the Ewells' activities." Dumbfounded, Scout can only accept Atticus' explanation.

Literary Device

Lee uses that explanation as *foreshadowing*—a literary device that alludes to something that will happen later in the story—of Mayella Ewell's reliance on special consideration for the accusations she brings against Tom Robinson. (Readers should note, too, that Lee masterfully keeps Boo Radley in the back of readers' minds by commenting that Scout "passed the Radley Place for the fourth time that day—twice at full gallop," while developing other major themes.)

Must be accepting of others' shortcomings. From Scout's perspective, all people, regardless of their station in life, are held to the same standards. Consequently, she feels perfectly justified in commenting on Walter Cunningham's table manners. Calpurnia takes her to task saying, "'Don't matter who they are, anybody sets foot in this house's yo' comp'ny, and don't you let me catch you remarkin' on their ways like you was so high and mighty!'" Adding insult to injury, Atticus agrees with Calpurnia.

Interestingly, in spite of Scout's protests that Walter Cunningham "made me start off on the wrong foot," her friendship with him will later save Atticus in a potentially life-threatening situation.

The art of compromise. Despite Atticus' probing questions about Scout's first day of school, she says little. Scout is despondent at the thought of not being able to read at home anymore, but reluctant to tell Atticus after the trouble she's been in all day. Atticus is quite understanding and suggests a compromise: "'If you'll concede the necessity of going to school, we'll go on reading every night just as we always have.'" Surprisingly, Atticus asks that she keep their deal a secret from Miss Caroline, introducing Scout to the idea of a white lie. Throughout the story, Atticus functions as a peacemaker. Lee gives the reader a first glimpse into Atticus' reasoning abilities and personal beliefs in his choice to compromise with Scout rather than confront or ignore Miss Caroline.

Glossary

Big Mules political term referring to modern Alabama power brokers.

catawba worms a type of caterpillar highly prized by fishermen in the Southern United States.

Lorenzo Dow a fiery, itinerant Methodist preacher of the Eastern and Southern United States.

hookworms a disease caused by hookworms, characterized by anemia, weakness, and abdominal pain: the larvae enter the body through the skin, usually of the bare feet.

entailment the act of entailing or of giving, as an estate, and directing the mode of descent. In this case, Walter Cunningham is most likely in a dispute over who is rightful heir to a piece of property.

the crash the 1929 stock market crash, which gave rise to the period of the Great Depression.

WPA a part of Franklin D. Roosevelt's New Deal, the Works Progress Administration (WPA) built new roads, hospitals, and schools throughout America.

cootie [Slang] common head lice.

fractious peevish; irritable; cross.

magnesia a white, tasteless powder, used as a mild laxative and antacid.

Chapters 4 and 5

Summary

The school year passes slowly for Scout. Her grade is released a half hour earlier than Jem's, so Scout has to pass Boo Radley's house by herself every afternoon. One day, Scout notices something shiny in a tree at the edge of the Radley yard. When she goes back to investigate, she finds a stick of gum. Jem admonishes her for taking the gum, but Scout continues to check the knothole daily. On the last day of school, she and Jem find some coins in the tree, which they decide to keep until the next school year starts.

Dill arrives two days later to spend the summer. After an argument with Scout, Jem suggests they play a new game called "Boo Radley," which Scout recognizes as Jem's attempt to prove his bravery. Against Scout's better judgement, they enact Boo's life with great gusto until Atticus learns of the game. The children play the game less frequently after that, and Jem and Dill begin excluding Scout, spending more and more time together in the treehouse. Lonely, Scout begins spending more of her time with Miss Maudie.

When Scout insists that the boys include her in their plans, they tell her that they're going to deliver a note to Boo Radley asking him to come outside. She and Dill are posted as guards, while Jem tries to deliver the note, but Atticus intervenes, telling the children to leave the Radleys alone.

Commentary

As Scout finishes her first year of school, Harper Lee expands on several of the novel's central themes.

Education. Scout's real education occurs outside of school, as it does throughout the story. Scout herself recognizes this fact at some level when she says, "As for me, I knew nothing except what I gathered from *Time* magazine and reading everything I could lay hands on at home, but as I inched sluggishly along the treadmill of the Maycomb County school system, I could not help receiving the impression that I was being cheated out of something." Scout not only learns more outside of school, but the things she learns are also more important.

Prejudice. When Jem suggests that the knothole in the Radley's oak is an adult's hiding place, Scout corrects him, saying, "'Grown folks don't have hidin' places.'" Jem and Scout discover later in the book that many adults hide behind their prejudices, religious beliefs, and their personal notions of right and wrong.

Miss Maudie is one of the most open-minded residents of Maycomb, and true to her more liberal leanings, she even likes the weeds in her garden. Her feelings about plants are symbolic of the way some townspeople feel about others. Scout reports that her neighbor "loved everything that grew in God's earth, even the weeds. With one exception: If she found a blade of nut grass in her yard it was like the Second Battle of the Marne because "'one sprig of nut grass can ruin a whole yard.'" Metaphorically, the Ewells are a blade of nutgrass in the Maycomb community. Some of the town's residents would also say that the African Americans who live in Maycomb are blades of nutgrass that should be eradicated from "their" yard. These perceptions become important as the story progresses.

The blacks and whites separate themselves from each other by their speech—and at some level by their superstitions. When Jem tells Dill about Hot Steams, Scout says, "'Don't you believe a word he says, Dill, . . . Calpurnia says that's nigger-talk.'" Calpurnia, an African-American herself, doesn't want the white Finch children to talk like most of the black community does or to buy into their superstitions. Granted, Calpurnia is more educated than the majority of her peers, but it still seems unusual that she doesn't want the children emulating that speech or those beliefs.

Calpurnia's attitude about the way the Finch children should speak shows that she, too, separates whites from blacks. Calpurnia is teaching the children to be white, just as she taught her own son, Zeebo, to interact appropriately with the African-American community. Keep in mind that Calpurnia's actions do not necessarily mean that she agrees with this separation; she is simply acting in a way that is consistent with life in the southern United States during this time period.

Bravery. When Jem creates the Boo Radley game, Scout says, "Jem's head at times was transparent: he had thought that up to make me understand he wasn't afraid of Radleys in any shape or form, to contrast his own fearless heroism with my cowardice." As noted before, the concept of bravery is very important to Jem, and he cultivates it as much as he can. He has moved from weakly accepting a dare to touch the Radley house to retrieving a tire from the Radley yard to creating a game in which the children take on the personas of various Radley family members.

Jem's bravery increases when he and Dill decide to deliver the note to Boo. Scout, though, comically points out that Jem is not quite as brave as he fancies himself to be when she exclaims, "'Anybody who's brave enough to go up and touch the house hadn't oughta use a fishin' pole, . . . Why don't you just knock the front door down?'" a sentiment Atticus later echoes a little less humorously.

Dill's part in getting a note to Boo presents a different side of the bravery issue. Sometimes, having someone else do the dirty work is less frightening—a belief that gives mob mentality its start. Dill admits almost gleefully that the whole plan is his idea, yet Jem is the person taking the greater risk. This mentality will play out in the adult world during Tom Robinson's trial.

Trust. At this point in the story, Scout's world is a safe place—her greatest fears are largely products of her own imagination. So even though she is terrified to pass by the Radley house, she takes the gum she finds in their tree. Comically, Scout reports, "The gum looked fresh. . . . I licked it and waited for a while. When I did not die I crammed it into my mouth." As Scout moves from innocence or naiveté to maturity—part of a coming-of-age story—she will learn that she can't always trust those things that appear safe.

The children are beginning to understand this concept on an almost subconscious level. In comparing Miss Maudie to a seemingly more virtuous neighbor, Scout says, "she did not go about the neighborhood doing good, as did Miss Stephanie Crawford. But while no one with a grain of sense trusted Miss Stephanie, Jem and I had considerable faith in Miss Maudie." The clear differences between the things that Miss Stephanie does and the things she says are another indication to the children that things are not always what they seem.

Truth. Hand-in-hand with the issue of trust is that of truth. In the course of the novel, almost every character lies at some point. Although most of the lies are meant to keep people out of trouble, some of these untruths will have dire consequences for the town as a whole.

Scout is clear that "Dill Harris could tell the biggest ones I ever heard." Overall, Dill's lies are harmless, but during his summers in Maycomb, Scout gets her first lessons in discerning truth and recognizing fiction. When Scout questions Miss Maudie about the Boo Radley myths, Miss Maudie states "'That is three-fourths colored folks and one-fourth Stephanie Crawford,'" introducing Scout to the fact that "big ones" aren't limited to children.

Scout also begins to understand that sometimes people stretch the truth to get what they want. Jem tells Dill and Scout that if Atticus specifically says they can't play the Boo Radley game, he "had thought of a way around it." The fact that Scout is uneasy about "thinking of a way around it" foreshadows the severity of the lies told later in the story.

Ironically, Atticus, who throughout the story upholds truth, is the person who dupes Jem into admitting the real purpose of the Boo Radley game.

Femininity. Introduced in these chapters, the issue of femininity and women's roles in Maycomb society is a significant theme in *To Kill a Mockingbird.*

Jem criticizes Scout for acting like a girl, frequently making statements like "'I swear, Scout, sometimes you act so much like a girl it's mortifyin'.'"

Scout experiences a plight familiar to many women of that era when Dill proposes marriage: "He staked me out, marked me as property, said I was the only girl he would ever love, then he neglected me." This sense of people as property will play out in serious ways as the story progresses.

In these chapters, Lee makes mention of four very different kinds of women: Calpurnia, Miss Maudie, Miss Stephanie, and Mrs. Dubose. (Note that the only adult the children don't refer to as Miss or Mrs. is Calpurnia, who is black.)

Scout will face many forms of femininity as she tries to understand what it means to "be a girl." Importantly, Scout most closely identifies with Miss Maudie, "a chameleon lady who worked in . . . an old straw hat and men's coveralls, but after her five o'clock bath she would appear on the porch . . . in magisterial beauty." As the story progresses, Scout will drift toward adopting Miss Maudie's brand of feminine behavior.

Glossary

scuppernongs   a golden-green grape of the Southern U.S.

foot-washing Baptist   rural missionary Baptists who essentially take the Bible literally.

Chapters 6 and 7

Summary

On Dill's last night in Maycomb, he and Jem decide to "peep in the window with the loose shutter to see if they could get a look at Boo Radley." Scout discourages them from going to the Radley house, but reluctantly decides to join them. Someone inside the Radley house comes out and fires a shotgun. The children scurry out of the yard, but Jem gets caught on the fence and is forced to remove his pants to get to safety.

As the neighborhood gathers to discuss the gunfire, Dill concocts an unlikely explanation for Jem's lack of pants. Atticus tells Jem to get his pants from Dill and come home. At home, Jem confides in Scout that he's going back to the Radley's to get his pants. Scout literally fears for his life, but Jem would rather risk life and limb than admit to Atticus that he lied.

School starts again. This year, Jem and Scout walk home together, and they again begin finding things in the Radley's tree. After receiving several increasingly valuable treasures, Jem and Scout decide to write a thank-you note to whoever is leaving the gifts. When they try to deliver the note, however, they find to their dismay that the knothole has been filled with cement.

Commentary

These two chapters mark several endings and beginnings for Jem and Scout in terms of understanding. Chapter 6 concludes their second summer with Dill, while Chapter 7 begins Scout's second year of school. The reader should remember that the first sentence in Chapter 1 states that Scout is retelling the events that lead up to Jem's broken arm. These two chapters lay much of the remaining foundation for what is to come by further exploring the children's relationship—or lack thereof—with Boo Radley and his family.

Prejudice begins to play a bigger role in the novel in these two chapters. Truthfully, it is a kind of prejudice that spurs Jem and Dill to try to "get a look" at Boo Radley. All along they claim that their interest is in the name of friendship, but readers know by now that both boys have a morbid curiosity to gawk at what they assume must be a freak of nature.

The boys show prejudice toward Scout by saying things like, "'You don't have to come along, Angel May.'" They attribute her resistance to their plan as girlish behavior, when Scout is actually more rational about the situation.

Character Insight

Finally, prejudice appears when the neighbors comment that "'Mr. Radley shot at a Negro in his collard patch.'" Neither Mr. Radley nor the neighbors have any evidence that the trespasser was black; they make that assumption based on their perceptions of African Americans. The low station blacks hold in Maycomb is further revealed when Mr. Radley vows to aim low at the next trespasser, "'be it dog, [or] nigger.'" With this statement, blacks are relegated to the worth of an animal. Ironically, Atticus will later deal directly with a mad dog and a black man. How he handles each situation gives true insight into his moral code.

The truth becomes a blur in these chapters. Dill makes up a fantastic story as to why Jem lost his pants. The neighbors accept the story readily, although Atticus asks some questions that lead readers to believe he may suspect otherwise. Later, Mr. Radley tells Jem that he cemented the knot-hole because the "'Tree's dying.'" Mr. Radley and Jem both know that the tree is fine and that the hole is plugged to stop Jem and Scout from retrieving any more treasures. However, Jem is forced to accept that explanation when Atticus says, "'I'm sure Mr. Radley knows more about his trees than we do.'"

Jem's bravery reaches new heights in these chapters. He puts himself in peril three times: trying to peek in the Radley's window, helping Scout and Dill get to safety, and returning to the Radley yard to retrieve his pants. In the last instance, pride drives his bravery more than fear of punishment. Scout recommends that Jem deal with the punishment for lying rather than risk his life, but Jem insists, "'Atticus ain't ever whipped me since I can remember. I wanta keep it that way.'" Although Scout doesn't understand Jem's thinking, she does realize that Jem would rather lose his life than disappoint his father.

A major shift occurs in Jem that night, and in an attempt to understand this change, Scout, significantly, tries "to climb into Jem's skin and walk around in it." A second, and equally important, shift occurs in Jem when he begins to realize exactly why Mr. Radley cemented the knot-hole in what he and Scout now referred to as their tree. With this harsh realization, Jem moves one step closer to adulthood.

Again, these two chapters show Scout and Jem that appearances aren't always what they seem. They rightly conclude that someone is deliberately leaving gifts for them in the knothole, but they can't understand why this donor won't make himself known. After hearing Mr. Radley's stance on trespassers, Jem tells Scout in amazement that his pants "'were folded across the fence . . . like they were expectin' me.'" No one would dare go into the Radley yard after the gunfire, but who in the Radley house would fold Jem's pants without confronting either him or Atticus? They discover that some adults would rather lie than be frank with them. Jem's reaction to cementing the knothole would've been entirely different had Mr. Radley admitted that he didn't want anyone leaving or taking things from his property. The Radleys remain a mystery to them.

Scout is faced again with the issue of femininity. When the boys reluctantly allow her to join them on their peeping-Tom mission, Scout continues to voice reservations. Jem puts a halt to her reasoning by saying, "'I declare to the Lord you're gettin' more like a girl every day!'" Acting like a girl is no compliment, and Scout feels thrust into the role of co-conspirator.

Gender roles are still clearly defined in these chapters. When Jem tells Scout that his pants were sewn up when he retrieved them, he's careful to relate, "'Not like a lady sewed 'em, like somethin' I'd try to do.'" Not untypical of 1930s America, women are expected to sew well, men aren't. These clearly defined roles are often what Scout rebels against. Jem believes that whomever is leaving gifts in the tree is a man. Scout initially disagrees, but he convinces her that the mystery person is male. From Scout's perspective, the gift bearer is more likely to be a woman, but that idea is soon stifled.

This world is still one in which men don't cry. When Jem discovers the cemented knothole, his immediate response is, "'Don't you cry, now, Scout.'" Scout is surprised to find the cement in the tree, but she never shows any indication of tears. Jem, however, spends many tears on this loss, leading readers to believe that he was convincing himself, not Scout, not to cry. Jem cries because a silent friendship that was cemented figuratively through little gifts in a knothole has been ended—ended before he has a chance to say thank you—by someone else's decision to literally cement the tree. Curiously, Jem, though demonstrating a new-found maturity, shows what are thought to be more feminine emotions, while Scout grapples to understand why he's so upset.

Glossary

Kudzu a fast-growing, hairy perennial vine of the pea family, with large, three-part leaves: sometimes planted in the South for soil stabilization or forage.

Franklin stove a cast-iron heating stove resembling an open fireplace, named for Benjamin Franklin who invented it.

hoodoo bad luck, or a person or thing that causes bad luck.

Chapters 8 and 9

Summary

For the first time in decades, Maycomb gets snow. School is closed, so Jem and Scout spend their day trying to build a snowman. That night, Miss Maudie's house burns to the ground. Jem and Scout are sent to wait in front of the Radley's while the fire is still raging. Boo Radley walks up and puts a blanket around a shivering Scout's shoulders, but both she and Jem are too engrossed in the fire to notice. The next day, Scout is surprised to find Miss Maudie in good spirits, working in her yard and talking about expanding her garden.

Near Christmastime, a classmate taunts Scout with the news that Atticus is defending a black man. Atticus asks Scout to promise to "'hold your head high, and keep those fists down. . . . Try fighting with your head for a change,'"—a promise Scout tries to uphold, with limited success. Uncle Jack Finch comes for Christmas as he does every year; Scout and her family spend Christmas at Finch's Landing with Aunt Alexandra and her family. Alexandra's grandson, Francis, begins teasing Scout about Atticus defending a black man. She attacks Francis and is punished by Uncle Jack, who had warned her not to fight or curse. Christmas evening, she and Uncle Jack talk, and she explains to him where he went wrong in his discipline. The chapter ends as Scout overhears Atticus and Uncle Jack talking about Tom Robinson's trial, which will start soon.

Commentary

Lee introduces a great deal of symbolism in Chapters 8 and 9. When Scout sees the snow, a very unusual phenomenon in Alabama, she screams, "'The world's endin', Atticus! Please do something—!'" Atticus is reassuring, but, importantly, from this point on in the story, Scout's world as she knows it does end. After Chapter 8, everything Scout believes turns topsy-turvy, and the things she takes as absolutes are going to come into question.

Jem's quest to build a snowman requires some ingenuity on his part. He first constructs a mudman, prompting Scout to say, "'Jem, I ain't ever heard of a nigger snowman.'" But Jem proceeds to cover the mudman with snow, making him white. In some ways their snowman is analogous to the way blacks are treated in Maycomb. Blacks aren't judged on their own merits, but on their relationships with the white folks in town, just as the mudman isn't something to be admired until he is a white snowman. Lee subtly and masterfully drives this point home by having the children create a nearly exact replica of Mr. Avery, a white neighbor who behaves crudely and indecently, unlike any black character in the story.

Lee also introduces bird symbolism into the novel in Chapter 8. When Miss Maudie's house catches fire, Scout says, "Just as the birds know where to go when it rains, I knew when there was trouble in our street." Bird imagery continues throughout the novel to be a pivotal symbol for sensing, and then doing, the right thing. (Readers should note the connection between Lee's use of bird symbolism and Atticus' last name, Finch.)

In another nod to how their world is changing, Jem and Scout have a chance to meet Boo Radley, but are too absorbed in something else to notice. And, instead of seeing the blanket as a gift, Scout is sick to her stomach. Miss Maudie's reaction to the fire confuses the children as well. They can't understand how she can be so positive and interested in them when she's lost everything. The children don't realize that the cuts on Miss Maudie's hands are evidence of the grief she chooses not to show.

The fire itself is symbolic of the upcoming conflicts that Scout and the community will face. This jarring event awakens the neighborhood, and Scout, from their peaceful slumber. The heat of the fire contrasts sharply with the intense cold, providing an allusion to the sharply defined sides in the upcoming trial and conflict. Neither fires nor cold are common in Maycomb, and the community is forced to look at situations from a different perspective.

Lee is careful to make clear that the children don't mind Atticus defending a black man as much as they mind the comments other people make about Atticus. She makes her point beautifully when Jem suggests that Miss Maudie get a "colored man" to help her with her yard, and Scout then notes, "There was no note of sacrifice in his voice when he added, 'Or Scout 'n' me can help you.'"

Through dialogue in Chapter 9, Lee communicates that Atticus doesn't have a chance to win Tom Robinson's case, bringing the theme of justice to the forefront. Atticus tells Scout that he has to fight a battle he can't win because it is the morally correct thing to do. Atticus is accustomed to facing no-win situations.

To their delight, he buys both children air rifles for Christmas, but says, "'I merely bowed to the inevitable.'" Later in the story, Atticus also accepts that Scout and Jem will kill birds; still, he won't teach them to shoot. Likewise, he accepts the fact that the jury will convict Tom, but he still gives him a courageous defense. (Ironically, the Finch family owned slaves at one time, making Atticus' defense of Tom that much more noble.)

Lee foreshadows how the jury will treat Tom in Scout's confrontation with Uncle Jack. Uncle Jack punishes Scout without first hearing her side of the story. In her "trial," she was guilty until proven guilty. However, unlike Tom Robinson, Scout does win on appeal when she tells her uncle, "'you never stopped to gimme a chance to tell you my side of it—you just lit right into me,'" at which point he does listen to her story. Lee adeptly helps readers understand how Tom feels by having a child experience the same emotions.

Character Insight

Still, even after Scout's "acquittal," Uncle Jack continues to fumble with the truth by dodging Scout's request for a definition of "whorelady." Readers gain a better sense of Atticus' moral code when he reprimands his brother for not directly answering Scout's question: "'Jack! When a child asks you something, answer him . . . children . . . can spot an evasion quicker than adults, and evasion simply muddles 'em.'"

Lee uses Scout's run-in with Francis to foreshadow one more important event. Scout muses, "When stalking one's prey, it is best to take one's time," which is exactly what Bob Ewell does in his attempt to harm Jem and Scout.

The outside world continues to impose standards of femininity on Scout in Chapter 8 and 9. Readers get the impression that Uncle Jack is less upset by Scout's language than by the fact that a girl is using that kind of language.

Scout doesn't want to "be a lady," but that doesn't stop her extended family from telling her she should be. Aunt Alexandra is more rigid about Scout's appearance than her male relatives. She abhors the idea of a little girl wearing pants and works diligently to make Scout more ladylike.

Curiously, Atticus comforts Scout by telling her that "Aunt Alexandra didn't understand girls much, she'd never had one." And more curious still is that the fact that Scout's not wanting to be a lady doesn't prevent her from also assigning gender roles as evidenced by her reaction to Francis learning to cook.

Glossary

aberrations a deviation from the normal or the typical.

touchous [Dial.] touchy.

thrift any of a genus of dwarf, evergreen, perennial dicotyledonous plants (order Plumbaginales) with narrow leaves and small, white, pink, red, or purplish flowers.

Appomattox town in central Virginia., near Lynchburg: In a former nearby village (Appomattox Court House), Lee surrendered to Grant (April 9, 1865), ending the Civil War.

caricatures a picture or imitation of a person, literary style, etc. in which certain features or mannerisms are exaggerated for satirical effect.

morphodite comic slang pronunciation of hermaphrodite, a term used to describe a human or animal combining both male and female sexual characteristics or organs.

Missouri Compromise a plan agreed upon by the United States Congress in 1820 to settle the debate over slavery in the Louisiana Purchase area. The plan temporarily maintained the balance between free and slave states.

Ol' Blue Light nickname for Stonewall Jackson, a Confederate general.

lineaments any of the features of the body, usually of the face, esp. with regard to its outline.

hookah a kind of water pipe associated with the Middle East, with a long flexible tube for drawing the smoke through water in a vase or bowl and cooling it.

trousseau a bride's outfit of clothes, linens, etc.

deportment the manner of conducting or bearing oneself; behavior; demeanor.

obstreperous noisy, boisterous, or unruly, esp. in resisting or opposing.

ruination anything that ruins or causes ruin.

Chapters 10 and 11

Summary

Jem and Scout lament the fact that "Atticus was feeble: he was nearly fifty." The children believe that Atticus' "advanced" age keeps him from doing the sorts of things other children's fathers do. Their view of their father changes when they see him shoot a mad dog.

As Tom Robinson's trial grows closer, Jem and Scout endure more slurs against their father. When their neighbor Mrs. Dubose, a mean, elderly woman confined to a wheel chair, makes a particularly stinging remark, Jem retaliates by destroying some of her flowers. Of course, Atticus hears what happened and he makes Jem apologize to Mrs. Dubose, letting her decide his punishment. Jem is sentenced to read to Mrs. Dubose after school for one month. Scout chooses to accompany Jem. Shortly after Jem is relieved from duty, Mrs. Dubose dies. Only then does Atticus tell the children that Mrs. Dubose was very sick and fighting an extremely valiant battle against addiction.

Commentary

The last two chapters of Part One complete the background for the trial that is coming in Part Two. Scout and Jem learn some impressive things about their father—things that will ultimately help them understand why Atticus is compelled to defend Tom Robinson. The children also confront ugliness and hostility, only to find that the reason behind the behavior follows the ethical high ground.

The title of *To Kill a Mockingbird* is explained in Chapter 10. When Atticus procures air guns for Scout and Jem, he warns them to "'remember it's a sin to kill a mockingbird.'" This statement surprises Scout—Atticus doesn't make a habit of saying that things are sinful. Scout takes her confusion to Miss Maudie who explains, "'mockingbirds . . . don't do one thing but sing their hearts out for us.'" Boo Radley and Tom Robinson are both mockingbirds in this story, but Scout doesn't realize that fully until the end of the novel.

Beyond the mockingbird image, Lee continues bird symbolism in the case of the bird dog, Tim Johnson. Tim is "the pet of Maycomb," but one day the children discover him acting strangely. Calpurnia confirms that the dog is very sick, and consequently, very dangerous. Although the children recognize that the dog's behavior is odd, he doesn't look mad to them. Mad dogs are supposed to have certain characteristics, as Scout testifies when she says, "Had Tim Johnson behaved thus, I would have been less frightened." Significantly, Scout will learn that the town behaves much like Tim Johnson during Tom's trial. They appear to be the same, but danger lurks beneath. More significant still is that as Tim approaches the neighborhood, even the mockingbirds become still.

Through Tim Johnson, Jem and Scout gain further insight into their father, just as they will through Tom Robinson's trial. To their delight, Jem and Scout discover that Atticus was nicknamed One-Shot Finch as a boy. Jem and Scout can't understand why Atticus doesn't continue to use his innate talent for hunting like other men in Maycomb do. Again, the children take their confusion to Miss Maudie who explains, "'I think maybe he put his gun down when he realized that God had given him an unfair advantage over most living things.'" Atticus is simply unwilling to take advantage of something that can't fight back. In fact, he feels that his talent for shooting demands that he be more careful and thoughtful about those unable to fight. This stance is one of the reasons that Atticus must defend Tom, a black man helpless against the rifles of prejudice carried by many whites in Maycomb.

When Calpurnia tries to warn the Radleys about Tim Johnson's approach, Lee deftly keeps the lower-class status of blacks in the forefront by having Scout comment "'She's supposed to go around in back.'" Calpurnia is the closest thing to a mother that the Finch children have, but at a tender age, Scout recognizes that different rules apply to blacks and whites. The fact that she doesn't question these rules is not a character flaw on her part. In the American South during this time period, segregation was the law. Scout would not have any concept that these rules were demeaning or unfair, as is evidenced by her asking Atticus to define the term "nigger-lover" for her.

Jem and Scout are forced to once again alter their definition of bravery in these chapters, as well. When Atticus cheerily greets Mrs. Dubose, Scout believes him to "be the bravest man who ever lived." Ironically, then, Atticus tells his children that Mrs. Dubose "'was the bravest person I ever knew.'" The fact that someone so foul and mean could be brave is new to Jem and Scout. The children hate her until the moment Atticus explains her bravery to them.

Scout is proud that she has chosen to be a coward at Atticus' bequest by no longer fist fighting with children who make disparaging remarks. So Atticus' statement that "'real courage is . . . when you know you're licked before you begin but you begin anyway and you see it through no matter what'" is a revelation to Scout as well as Jem.

This revelation also brings up the role of conscience in the novel, which Lee treats in a fairly overt manner. When Scout questions the sense in defending Tom, Atticus offers, "'Tom Robinson's case, is something that goes to the essence of a man's conscience— cout, I couldn't go to church and worship God if I didn't try to help that man.'" Although Jem's reaction to Mrs. Dubose's final gift to him seems strong, readers should understand that Jem is actually grappling with his conscience. After all the wicked things he's thought about Mrs. Dubose, he discovers the reasons behind her behavior were understandable, if not acceptable. Not only has Jem learned a new way of defining courage, but he is also forced to look at the motivations for his own actions.

The issues of masculinity and femininity continue to have a role in these chapters. Scout doesn't think it odd that Atticus buys an air rifle for her as well as Jem, although girls traditionally aren't sharpshooters. Jem's admiration for Atticus continues to grow, so much so that Jem begins to consider himself "a gentleman." Ironically, then, when Jem is cautioning Scout about reacting to Mrs. Dubose, instead of telling her to act like a lady, he says, "'Don't pay any attention to her, just hold your head high and be a gentleman.'" Later, Jem is completely shocked to hear Atticus refer to Mrs. Dubose as "a great lady" when both she and her mouth are so vile.

Glossary

philippic a bitter verbal attack.

umbrage offense or resentment.

interdict to prohibit (an action) or prohibit the use of (a thing); forbid with authority.

Dixie Howell popular University of Alabama football player in the 1930s.

palliation the lessening of pain or severity without actually curing; alleviation.

reconnaissance an exploratory survey or examination, as in seeking out information about enemy positions or installations, or as in making a preliminary geological or engineering survey.

calomel mercurous chloride, $HgCl$, a white, tasteless powder that darkens on exposure to light: used in standard electrode cells and in agriculture and medicine to fight skin bacteria.

Part Two
Chapters 12 and 13

Summary

As summer begins, Jem is now too old to be bothered by his little sister, which causes Scout great dismay. To add to Scout's disappointment, Dill won't be coming to Maycomb this summer, although Calpurnia eases her loneliness somewhat. With Atticus at a special session of the state legislature, Calpurnia takes the children to church with her. Upon their return from church, they find Aunt Alexandra waiting on the porch for them. She announces that at Atticus' request, she's coming to live with them for "a while." Aunt Alexandra goes to great pains to educate the children in the importance of the Finch breeding, going so far as to have Atticus deliver an uncharacteristic speech—a speech he ultimately recants—to Scout and Jem.

Commentary

The third and final summer chronicled in *To Kill a Mockingbird* begins in these chapters. With school out, Scout's real education will begin again. In fact, during this summer, she, Jem, and Dill will probably learn the most important and lasting lessons of their lives. Lee hints at this by noting the changes in Jem: he doesn't want Scout "pestering" him; Calpurnia begins referring to him as "Mister Jem," a title reserved for adults; and, he develops "a maddening air of wisdom" that only annoys Scout. She doesn't understand these changes, but the adults around her expect them.

The minor hardships that start the summer foreshadow the much bigger dilemmas that the children will face during Tom's trial and its aftermath. Scout loses Jem as a regular playmate, causing her to fume. Then Scout receives word that Dill is staying in Meridian this summer, and Atticus is called to an emergency session of the legislature. Finally, Aunt Alexandra arrives to live with them, seemingly unannounced. These small disappointments and challenges hint at the larger inconsistencies and unexpected outcomes of Tom Robinson's trial, which follows.

For some time now, Scout and Jem have railed against people who insulted Atticus' decision to defend Tom. However, in these chapters, they begin to understand the importance of other people's opinions about them, especially Aunt Alexandra who "never let a chance escape her to point out the shortcomings of other tribal groups to the glory of our own."

Calpurnia worries about what others think as well. She is fanatical about Jem and Scout's cleanliness and attire when she takes them to church with her because "'I don't want anybody sayin' I don't look after my children.'" Cal really does think of the Finch children as her children, yet she is black and they are white. The children don't understand prejudice at its basest level, and Calpurnia seems to not possess it either. Consequently, the children are surprised when they ironically experience prejudice while attending Calpurnia's church. There, a churchgoer named Lula confronts Calpurnia with, "'I wants to know why you bringin' white chillun to nigger church.'" Prejudice appears to run from black toward white as much as from white toward black. In this instance, the children are like mockingbirds—they're just there to please Calpurnia and worship. This experience will give the children more compassion toward Tom's treatment from a white jury. However, just as every white resident of Maycomb isn't prejudiced, not every member of Calpurnia's church is, either. Both Reverend Skyes and Zeebo are quite glad to have them and tell them so.

Style & Language

The children are further surprised to hear Calpurnia talk like other black people. Scout comments "The idea that she had a separate existence outside our household was a novel one, to say nothing of her having command of two languages." Significantly, Scout sees the language of the two races as different, but more importantly, she is impressed by Calpurnia's mastery of both. If Scout were raised in a prejudiced household, she would find this other "language" inferior.

In their childish innocence, Jem and Scout are surprised to find that only four people in Calpurnia's church can read. They have no understanding that for the most part, Maycomb's black population is denied an education. In fact, when Calpurnia remarks that black people don't age as quickly as white people, Jem seriously suggests, "'Maybe because they can't read'" as though reading is a burden that not everyone needs to shoulder. Lee uses the children's ignorance to underscore the injustice African Americans receive in all aspects of their lives. All white children—even the Ewells—are afforded the opportunity to learn to read. Scout and Jem's surprise helps readers understand this unfairness at a deeper level.

Remarkably, Calpurnia doesn't lament the African-American position in Maycomb society or try to explain prejudice to the children. Instead, she simply answers their questions, and lets them figure out the rest. When Scout asks to visit Calpurnia at her house, Calpurnia doesn't go into a dissertation about how white children generally don't spend time in black people's homes, she just smiles and says, "'We'd be glad to have you.'"

Ironically, Aunt Alexandra holds many of Maycomb's prejudices against blacks. She has an African-American chauffeur, and says "'Put my bag in the front bedroom, Calpurnia'" before she even says hello. The fact that Jem insists on taking the bag shows both maturity and lack of prejudice on his part.

Still, Aunt Alexandra's various prejudices cause Scout to comment "There was indeed a caste system in Maycomb, but to my mind it worked this way: the older citizens, the present generation of people who had lived side by side for years and years, were utterly predictable to one another." Later in the novel, Scout will redefine Maycomb's caste system as she discovers that even living "side by side for years and years" doesn't make human nature predictable.

Aunt Alexandra claims that the main reason she's come to live with them is to provide "some feminine influence" for Scout. Of course, Scout considers Calpurnia to be a sufficient feminine influence. Aunt Alexandra would be quick to say that the finest black woman can't ever be a proper role model for a white child.

In these chapters, Scout confronts the issue of femininity through others in her household, as well:

Jem and Atticus: In a major and unexpected shift, Jem stops chastising Scout for acting like a girl, and instead says, "'It's time you started bein' a girl and acting right!'" Scout is stunned to tears by this sudden change in Jem.

Later, Atticus further confuses the children by deeming that they need to start "'behaving like the little lady and gentleman that you are.'" Atticus quickly realizes that he doesn't mean what he's saying and withdraws his request for different behavior. He then tries to make light of the whole situation to cheer the children up. Curiously, Scout recognizes that "Atticus was only a man. It takes a woman to do that kind of work." So at the end of Chapter 13, readers are left with the impression that Scout is beginning to come to grips with what being female means.

Calpurnia: With much more gentle tactics than Aunt Alexandra, Calpurnia shows Scout a great deal about femininity.

Scout absorbs Calpurnia's lessons willingly because Calpurnia doesn't try to force any standards on her. Scout simply starts joining her in the kitchen as Jem enters adolescence and she remarks "by watching her I began to think there was some skill involved in being a girl." Ironically, although Aunt Alexandra wants to be Scout's example of the feminine, Scout chooses to follow the examples set by women like Miss Maudie and Calpurnia. Lee shows the juxtaposition between Calpurnia and Aunt Alexandra by the fact that Alexandra won't let Calpurnia cook for her lady friends.

Ironically, though, at Calpurnia's church, Scout is "confronted with the Impurity of Women doctrine." Reverend Skyes, like many others in the clergy, espouses the evils that women bring on the world, and yet everyone in the world seems to want to transform her into one of these creatures. It is indeed a confusing time for Scout.

Glossary

Shadrach *Bible* one of the three captives who came out of the fiery furnace miraculously unharmed: Dan. 3:12-27.

castile a fine, mild, hard soap prepared from olive oil and sodium hydroxide.

habiliments clothing; dress; attire.

Quarters a particular district or section in a city.

asafoetida a bad-smelling gum resin obtained from various Asiatic plants of the umbel family: it was formerly used to treat some illnesses or, in folk medicine, to repel disease.

church vt. to bring (esp. a woman after childbirth) to church for special services.

rotogravure a printing process using photogravure cylinders on a rotary press.

impedimenta things hindering progress, as on a trip; encumbrances; esp., baggage, supplies, or equipment, as those carried along with an army.

voile a thin, sheer fabric, as of cotton, used for garments, curtains, etc.

Blackstone's Commentaries one of the most important books ever written on British law, written by Sir William Blackstone 1723-80; Eng. jurist & writer on law.

tight [slang] drunk.

amanuensis an assistant who takes dictation or copies something already written; secretary.

redbug any of various red insects, as a cotton stainer or chigger.

Chapters 14 through 16

Summary

As Scout innocently recounts her trip to Calpurnia's church for Atticus, Aunt Alexandra is mortified and vehemently refuses Scout's request to go to Calpurnia's house. With Scout out of the room, she comments that they really don't need a housekeeper now that she's come to stay, recommending that Atticus let Calpurnia go. Now it's Atticus' turn to vehemently deny Alexandra's request. Jem and Scout retreat to let the adults work out their differences, but end up in a fistfight with each other. Sent to bed early, Jem and Scout get themselves ready for sleep. Crossing the floor in the darkened room, Scout feels what she thinks is a snake. Jem discovers that the "snake" is Dill with a fantastic story of his runaway voyage to Maycomb. Jem calls Atticus who arranges for Dill to spend the night.

Dill's mother gives him permission to spend the summer in Maycomb and the children begin to enjoy their time together. Then Sheriff Tate and a group of other men come by the house to tell Atticus that Tom Robinson is being moved to the county jail and that there may be trouble. That Sunday night, Atticus heads into town, which gives Jem a funny feeling. At bedtime, he, Scout, and Dill walk downtown themselves to see what's happening. They find Atticus sitting outside Tom Robinson's cell and turn to head home when a group of men arrive to confront Atticus. Not realizing the danger of the situation, Scout runs into the middle of the mob. After a few tense moments, she begins a conversation with Walter Cunningham's father, which causes the men to retreat, and very likely saves Atticus' life.

The next morning, the day the trial is set to begin, Atticus and Scout talk about mob mentality, and, over Aunt Alexandra's protests, he thanks the children for appearing when they did. He asks the children to stay away from the courthouse during the trial, but by noon, their curiosity has the better of them, and they, along with Dill, head for the courthouse where the trial is about to get underway. They can't find a seat in the courtroom, so Reverend Skyes offers them seats in "the Colored balcony," which they gladly accept. Finally, readers are introduced to Judge Taylor, who the children earlier discovered—much to their surprise—appointed Atticus to defend Tom Robinson.

Commentary

In these chapters, prejudice comes to the forefront in numerous ways. Aunt Alexandra refuses to allow Scout to visit Calpurnia because young white girls don't spend time in black people's neighborhoods, and definitely not inside their houses. In fact, Aunt Alexandra thinks that Atticus should terminate Calpurnia's employment with the family. Significantly, Atticus defends Calpurnia, saying, "'I don't think the children have suffered one bit from her having brought them up. If anything, she's been harder on them in some ways than a mother would've been.'" If the thought hasn't occurred to readers by now, they're confronted with the fact that for all the prejudices African Americans endure, Atticus has allowed a black woman to raise his children, and in fact, sees this woman as "a faithful member of this family." Atticus' attitude is certainly atypical of the Maycomb majority.

Atticus' attitude toward African Americans is further exposed the morning after he faces the mob at the jailhouse. Aunt Alexandra chastises him for remarking that Mr. Underwood "despises Negroes" in front of Calpurnia. But characteristically, Atticus responds, "'Anything fit to say at the table's fit to say in front of Calpurnia.'" Aunt Alexandra is afraid that the black community will gossip about the white community, but Atticus proclaims that maybe the white community shouldn't give them so much to gossip about. While Alexandra worries about appearances, Atticus constantly reminds her of reality.

In the American South during the 1930s, segregation was not only the norm, it was the law. Blacks were given special places to sit, they often used separate entrances, and they used separate restrooms and drinking fountains. The fact that blacks can't sit on the main floor of the courtroom or that they have to let all the white people into the courthouse before they can begin going in themselves, is an accurate description of what would've happened at such a trial. When Reverend Skyes offers the children a seat in the "Colored balcony," they happily and naively accept. They have no idea that they're breaking a cultural taboo. Many whites would miss the trial before they would sit amongst people of another race. Ironically, Scout feels like they have a better view from the balcony than they would from the floor—unfortunately, what they're going to see won't be pretty. Significant, too, is that four black people rose to give the minister and three white children their front-row seats. Some would argue that they gave up their seats out of respect for Reverend Skyes; others may say that they gave up their seats out of respect for Atticus. In truth, they would be expected to give up their seats for any white person who wanted them.

Lee introduces an interesting discussion of what makes a person a member of one race or another through the character of Dolphus Raymond—a white man, rumored to be a drunkard, with biracial children. Worse than being black is being "mixed." Children who are part of both races "don't belong anywhere. Colored folks won't have 'em because they're half white; white folks won't have 'em 'cause they're colored, so they're just in-betweens, don't belong anywhere."

When Jem points out some biracial children, Scout can't tell that they're "mixed" and wonders, then, how Jem knows that they aren't also mixed. Jem has discussed this topic with Uncle Jack, who says that they may have some black ancestors several generations back. Somewhat relieved, Scout determines that after so many generations, race doesn't count, but Jem says, "'around here once you have one drop of Negro blood, that makes you all black.'" This conversation is important because Jem and Scout accept the idea that they themselves could have a "drop of Negro blood," which makes them more open to the African-American community and less prejudiced than the vast majority of Maycomb.

The importance of place again comes to light in these chapters. As the children watch the town heading for the courthouse, "Jem gave Dill the histories and general attitudes of the more prominent figures." Again, Dill becomes an important vehicle for the children to understand their own community. What they take for granted is news to Dill, which forces them to look at their town in a different light.

Place is also important in the sense that Dill feels compelled to return to Maycomb, even though that means running away from home. Dill is unhappy with his new stepfather, but readers sense that summers in Maycomb have become part of Dill's sense of place. After two summers in Maycomb, he belongs there. Maycomb may not be a very nice town to live in if you aren't white, but for Dill, the town is a sanctuary when things are stormy elsewhere. For Scout, Maycomb and her family are as much a part of her as her own skin. Listening to Dill's reasons for leaving his home, Scout "found myself wondering . . . what I would do if Atticus did not feel the necessity of my presence, help and advice. . . . Even Calpurnia couldn't get along unless I was there. They needed me." The idea that someone can be unwanted in a place where they supposedly belong is completely foreign to Scout. Later, she and

Dill discuss why Boo Radley has never run away—he surely must not feel wanted. Dill muses that he must not have a safe haven "to run off to."

In these chapters, Lee uses Dill and Jem to show the contrast between childish innocence and adult maturity. Dill shows the last vestige of childhood innocence by being the only one of the three still scheming to get Boo Radley out of his house. By suggesting that a trail of candy will make Boo leave his home, Dill still applies methods that would appeal to children, not adults. Jem demonstrates a new level of understanding when he refuses to keep Dill's presence a secret from Atticus. Though calling Atticus means incurring the wrath of his peers, Jem realizes that Dill's family is also concerned.

Jem also moves one step closer to adulthood when he refuses to obey his father for the first time in his life. Scout explains, "In the midst of this strange assembly, Atticus stood trying to make Jem mind him. 'I ain't going,' was his steady answer." Scout recognizes that Jem is exhibiting great courage, but only after the fact does she realize that Jem and his father have moved to a new level in their relationship with each other.

Scout attempts to keep up with Jem and his newfound wisdom— and is, in fact, headed toward a new level of maturity herself—but Jem's treatment of her makes clear to the reader that Scout is still very much a child, as yet incapable of understanding many of life's complex issues. Lee's reinforcement of Scout's childishness in these chapters is a device that allows Scout the complete objectivity of a child while recounting the difficult events and issues that later surface in the trial.

Bravery takes on a new role as the children face the mob threatening Atticus at the jail. Recognizing Atticus' bravery in going to the courthouse in the first place, Jem shows his bravery by refusing to leave his father with the group of men. Scout, however, is braver by addressing the mob, although, ironically, she has no idea how brave she's being. Not until she's safely tucked in bed that night does Scout realize that the line between bravery and foolhardiness is thin. Significantly, Dill is quiet throughout the entire confrontation with the mob. He simply absorbs what he sees and hears, which foreshadows how he will perceive Tom's trial.

At breakfast the morning after the showdown at the jail, Scout and Jem are full of questions about why people act the way they do. They can't understand why Atticus isn't angry at the men who were ready to hurt him and lynch Tom. But, in his usual way, Atticus explains that people don't always act in attractive or reasonable ways. Mobs take on a life of their own, but they're still composed of people. He then goes on to imply that children are sometimes better judges of a situation than adults by saying, "'maybe we need a police force of children . . . you children made Walter Cunningham stand in my shoes for a minute. That was enough.'"

On the day of the trial, people crawl out of the woodwork to attend. Some are simply curious, but most are coming to make sure that justice is served, and the only justice they can accept is a conviction for Tom Robinson. The children get more insight into Miss Maudie's feelings about the trial and her distaste for mob mentality when she tells them that she has "'no business with the court this morning. . . . 't's morbid, watching a poor devil on trial for his life. Look at all those folks, it's like a Roman carnival.'" Miss Maudie shows great fortitude by refusing to participate in what is bound to be a debacle.

Lee provides an interesting look at the issue of femininity in these chapters. First, Atticus and Aunt Alexandra debate "southern womanhood." Later, when facing the mob at the jail, Scout acts like anything but a Southern woman when she kicks one of the men for insulting Jem. Ironically, then, Scout is called a lady for the first time when Walter Cunningham says, "'I'll tell him you said hey, little lady.'" With this turn of events, Lee suggests that "southern womanhood" is a myth—Scout is developing into a bright, well-mannered young woman, but she certainly doesn't fit the stereotype of a delicate, refined belle.

Glossary

johnson grass a forage and pasture grass, widespread in the Southern U.S., often as a weed.

monkey-puzzle bushes any araucaria tree; esp., a tall tree with stiff pointed leaves, edible nuts, and hard wood, widely grown as an ornamental.

ecclesiastical of the church, the organization of the church, or the clergy.

privy a toilet; esp., an outhouse.

acquiescence the act of acquiescing; agreement or consent without protest.

snipe hunt   practical joke in which the victim is made to sit in the woods with a bag and two sticks in an attempt to capture a creature that doesn't exist.

aggregation   a group or mass of distinct things or individuals.

fey   strange or unusual in any of certain ways, as, variously, eccentric, whimsical, visionary, elfin, shy, otherworldly.

Braxton Bragg   Commander of the Confederate Army of Tennessee from the summer of 1862 until the end of 1863. Bragg had the distinction of being both recklessly offensive as well as hesitant to the point of ineffectiveness at various times in his career—sometimes in the same battle.

popped-the-whip   this is in reference to a game in which a group of children line up together hand-in-hand; one end of the line slings itself forward, causing the child at the other end of the line to receive a violent snap.

solicitor   in the U.S., a lawyer serving as official law officer for a city, department, etc..

champertous   having to do with champerty, an act by which a person not concerned in a lawsuit makes a bargain with one of the litigants to help maintain the costs of the suit in return for a share of any proceeds: illegal in most U.S. states.

Chapters 17 through 20

Summary

The trial begins. Heck Tate is the first witness. Under cross-examination, he admits that a doctor was never called to the scene to examine Mayella Ewell. Bob Ewell takes the stand next and causes a stir in the courtroom with his bad attitude and foul language. Mr. Ewell is not shaken from his story, but Atticus carefully plants the seed that Mr. Ewell himself could've beaten Mayella. Mayella takes the stand next. Even though Atticus believes that she's lying, he treats her with courtesy and respect; Mayella thinks that he's making fun of her. Her testimony soon proves that Mayella is unused to gentility and common courtesy. Atticus asks Tom to stand up so that Mayella may identify him; as he does, Scout notices that Tom's left arm is withered and useless—he could not have committed the crime in the way it was described. The state rests its case.

Atticus calls only one witness—Tom Robinson. Tom tells the true story, being careful all the while not to come right out and say that Mayella is lying. However, Tom makes a fatal error when he admits under cross-examination that he, a black man, felt sorry for Mayella Ewell. Dill has a very emotional response to Mr. Gilmer's questioning and leaves the courtroom in tears. Scout follows Dill outside, where they talk with Dolphus Raymond, who reveals the secret behind his brown bag and his drinking. Scout and Dill return to the courtroom in time to hear the last half of Atticus's impassioned speech to the jury. Just as Atticus finishes, Calpurnia walks into the courtroom and heads toward Atticus.

Commentary

At this point in the story, readers may be tempted to think that Tom Robinson's trial is basically about white prejudice against African Americans. Prejudice certainly does come to play in the court proceedings, but Lee explores much deeper human emotions and societal ideals than the straightforward mistreatment of a person based on skin color.

The Ewells are what people today would call "white trash." Scout sums the Ewells up when she says "people like the Ewells lived as guests of the county in prosperity as well as in the depths of depression. No truant officers could keep their numerous offspring in school; no public health officer could free them from congenital defects, various worms, and the diseases indigenous to filthy surroundings." The Ewells forage for food, furnishings, and water at the town dump, which is very close to their shack. Just beyond their home is a "Negro settlement." Atticus had once taken Scout and Jem out to the dump to discard their Christmas tree, and Scout noticed that the black people's houses were modest but neat and appeared to be clean with aromatic smells rising from their kitchens—quite a contrast to the Ewell's surroundings. The fact is that most in the African-American community live cleaner, more honest, and more productive lives than the Ewells. Consequently, the resentment against blacks on the part of the "white trash" runs deep.

Against this backdrop of a trial where a "white-trash" female is accusing a black man of a violent crime, Lee expertly explores several of the novel's major themes while focusing on the questions of prejudice and class or social station.

In Maycomb during the time of Tom Robinson's trial, African Americans reside at the bottom of the totem pole as far as power in the community. Even Scout, who probably can't yet define the term "prejudice," tells Dill, "'Well, Dill, after all, he's just a Negro.'" Scout's community has so reinforced the low station of blacks that she innocently accepts and helps maintain that station. In Scout's world, some things just are, and the fact that blacks are "just Negroes" is one of them. In fact, Scout shows her lack of intentional prejudice by admitting "If he [Tom Robinson] had been whole, he would have been a fine specimen of a man."

It is fair to assume, however, that the adult Scout who is actually telling the story has come to understand the error of thinking that any human being is lesser than another based solely on skin color. If Scout believed that blacks were truly lesser, then her character would have no reason for telling this story—the story she'd tell, if she told one at all, would be markedly different.

The blacks in the community accept their lot. They may not like the treatment they receive, but to defy the rules set by the community means literally risking their lives. Tom Robinson did nothing but help Mayella Ewell. In fact, he "was probably the only person who was ever decent to her." The only thing that Tom is guilty of is feeling sorry for

Mayella. But, for an African-American man to publicly admit feeling pity for *any* white person is overstepping societal bounds.

In truth, Tom embarrasses Mayella by refusing her advances and Mayella embarrasses her father by making advances toward a black man. Bob Ewell's pride can't afford for a black man to go back to his community talking about a white woman making a pass at him. Worse yet, Tom is now aware of incest in the Ewell household, something that is taboo in every class. Tom was unlikely to tell anyone of what had happened with Mayella, recognizing that his safety was at stake. Bob Ewell could've let the whole thing drop, but he'd rather be responsible for an innocent man's death than risk having his family further diminished in the town's eyes.

Truthfully, Tom's testimony actually embarrasses the Ewells more. Tom tells the court that Mayella asked him to kiss her saying, "'what her papa do to her don't count,'" which informs the whole town that Bob Ewell sexually abuses his daughter. He further tells the court that Bob called his own child a "goddamn whore." Tom is careful to never directly accuse Mayella of lying, repeatedly qualifying, "'she's mistaken in her mind.'"

Tom is a compassionate man, and ironically, his acts of kindness are responsible, at least indirectly, for his current situation. In Maycomb society (and, truthfully, the southern United States at this time), basic human kindness from a black person to a white person is impermissible. The consequences are deadly when the "lesser" show their compassion—and then have the audacity to admit it—for the "greater."

The all-white jury is in an awkward position. If they acquit a black man who admittedly pities a white person, then they're voting to lessen their own power over the black community. However, if they convict Tom, they do so knowing that they're sentencing an innocent man to death. Mayella makes their choice very easy when she looks at the jury and says, "'That nigger yonder took advantage of me an' if you fine fancy gentlemen don't wanta do nothin' about it then you're all yellow stinkin' cowards.'"

The remaining question about Tom's innocence is why did he run from the Ewell property if he did nothing wrong? Atticus explains that Tom was truly between a rock and a hard place: "he would not have dared strike a white woman under any circumstances and expect to live long, so he took the first opportunity to run—a sure sign of guilt." The rules are so clearly defined in favor of white people that Tom was literally doomed the moment Bob and Mayella Ewell decided to accuse him.

Dill, a child who has not yet reached Scout's level of acceptance about societal prejudices, reacts strongly to the lack of respect African Americans are shown. As Dill and Scout leave the courtroom for a few minutes, Dolphus Raymond explains his own disdain for "'the hell white people give colored folks, without even stopping to think that they're people, too.'" In fact, Raymond is so disturbed by this dichotomy that he prefers to live amongst black people; however, in order to save himself and his family from the same treatment that Tom is receiving, he pretends to be a drunkard. The white community excuses his behavior because they believe he is an alcoholic who "can't help himself." The thought has yet to occur to anyone that a white man may enjoy the company of African-American people. With that conversation, Scout is further educated about prejudice and the negative consequences that result from it.

When Bob Ewell takes the witness stand, Scout notes that the only thing "that made him better than his nearest neighbors was, that if scrubbed with lye soap in very hot water, his skin was white." It is ironic that the Ewells are so dirt-covered that identifying their skin color is difficult. Ewell testifies with the confidence of someone who knows he's already won. If his case weren't so clear cut in his eyes, he wouldn't make lewd jokes when being questioned on the witness stand.

The more sophisticated white people in Maycomb at least try to pretend that their prejudices don't run so deep, but Ewell is beyond this sort of genteel pretense. He boldly tells Judge Taylor that he's "'asked this county for fifteen years to clean out that nest down yonder, they're dangerous to live around 'sides devaluin' my property—'" If a man's life were not at stake, Ewell's testimony would be laughable. No one—not even a neighborhood of "lower-class" blacks—can devalue a piece of property that is basically an extension of the town dump. And, the entire courtroom will soon realize that the danger actually lies in living close to the Ewells, not vice versa.

Atticus gently shows the injustice of Tom's situation throughout the court proceedings. For instance, Atticus makes a point of noting that even though Mayella was badly beaten and claimed to have been brutally raped, no doctor was ever called to the scene. When he asks Sheriff Tate why he didn't call a doctor, the answer is a simple "'It wasn't necessary, Mr. Finch. . . . Something sho' happened, it was obvious.'" Of course, a doctor could have verified that Mayella had not been raped, and if a white man had been accused, a doctor almost surely would've been called. But Tom Robinson is a black man, so calling a doctor simply "wasn't necessary," another indicator of the deep-running prejudice that blacks in Maycomb live with every day.

Scout (as well as Judge Taylor) is genuinely surprised when Mayella claims that Atticus is mocking her. He is only treating her respectfully. That Lee chooses the word "mock" here is important. Mockingbirds repeat sounds they hear. They're like little echo machines. Atticus is only repeating the story as it really happened, but in this case, an echo is a very dangerous thing to Mayella. Lee describes Mayella as being like "a steady-eyed cat with a twitchy tail," which is ironic given that Tom is much like a mockingbird just trying to make her life easier and more enjoyable. Cats hunt birds, and Lee's description is of a cat stalking prey. After Mayella's testimony, Scout suddenly understands that Mayella is "even lonelier than Boo Radley."

During his closing argument, Atticus ties the questions of race and social station together. Making no judgement about Mayella, Atticus tells the jury that "'she has merely broken a rigid and time-honored code of our society, a code so severe that whoever breaks it is hounded from our midst as unfit to live with. . . . What did she do? She tempted a Negro.'" Atticus admits that like Tom Robinson, he pities Mayella Ewell, but Atticus is white and educated and so is allowed to feel that pity.

Had Tom Robinson been a woman accused of seducing a white man, the outcome of the trial would be no different. How then, is Dolphus Raymond allowed to live and procreate with black women? He's white, he owns land, and he comes from a "fine old family." Simply stated, the rules are different for a white male with this pedigree. Ironically, Scout thinks of Mayella as facing the same problems that a mixed child deals with: "white people wouldn't have anything to do with her because she lived among pigs; Negroes wouldn't have anything to do with her because she was white." Class can be as big a separator within a community as race.

Glossary

bantam cock a small but aggressive person; a bantam is a small domestic fowl.

crepey wrinkled like crepe cloth or paper.

acrimonious bitter and caustic in temper, manner, or speech.

ruttin' referring to rut, the periodic sexual excitement, or heat, of certain mammals: applied esp. to males.

tenet principle, doctrine, or belief held as a truth, as by some group.

ambidextrous able to use both hands with equal ease.

lavation the act of washing.

chiffarobe a wardrobe with drawers or shelves on one side.

frog-sticking a method of hunting frogs on bayou banks with a small pitchfork.

constructionist a person who interprets, or believes in interpreting, a law, document, etc. in a specified way.

ground-itch an itchy allergic reaction caused when parasitic hookworms enter the body through bare feet.

ex cathedra with the authority that comes from one's rank or office: often specif. with reference to papal pronouncements, on matters of faith or morals, regarded as having authoritative finality.

impudent shamelessly bold or disrespectful; saucy; insolent.

corroborative making certain; confirming; corroborating.

temerity foolish or rash boldness; foolhardiness; recklessness.

Chapters 21 through 23

Summary

Calpurnia brings a note telling Atticus that Scout and Jem are missing, which causes him great concern until Mr. Underwood tells him that the children are in the courtroom—in the Colored balcony. Calpurnia scolds the children all the way home, but Atticus says that they can return to hear the jury's verdict.

Jem is convinced that the jury will acquit Tom Robinson after the evidence Atticus presented. After the verdict, Jem leaves the courtroom stunned, angry, and crying. The African-American community loads the Finch family with food for defending Tom so valiantly, which surprises the children because Atticus didn't win. Atticus tells Jem not to be disheartened because he will appeal Tom's case, and they stand a much better chance of winning on appeal. The neighborhood is abuzz with talk of the trial, and Miss Stephanie questions the children relentlessly until Miss Maudie sides with Atticus and puts an end to the discussion.

In the days following the trial, Bob Ewell publicly threatens Atticus, which frightens the children. However, Atticus uses the opportunity to further educate his children on the ways of the world. As they look forward to the appeal, Scout asks if Walter Cunningham can come over to play, which Aunt Alexandra firmly refuses to allow. In the process, Aunt Alexandra hurts Scout's feelings horribly, prompting Jem to guess why Boo Radley chooses to stay inside.

Commentary

In these chapters, Scout and Jem continue to mature as they begin to understand the importance of respect and integrity. From the moment Atticus was assigned to defend Tom, he's been telling the children that he couldn't face them or God if he didn't try to free this man. But as the trial ends, the children gain new insight into their father. Scout is quite surprised when Reverend Skyes makes her stand along with the rest of the balcony as her father passes by. Lee deftly adds to the impact of the respect the African-American community has for Atticus by ending a chapter with this action.

The children are bitterly disappointed by the loss, but Miss Maudie helps them see it in a new light when she says, "'I thought, Atticus Finch won't win, he can't win, but he's the only man in these parts who can keep a jury out so long on a case like that.'" With that, the children begin to understand that in many ways, Atticus's defeat was a major victory.

The importance of respect is further delineated when Atticus tells the children that having a Cunningham on the jury actually helped his case, mainly because Scout earned Walter Cunningham's respect at the jail. And, Atticus changes Jem's definition of bravery, equating it with integrity, by his reaction to being spat on and threatened by Bob Ewell.

Mockingbird symbolism runs throughout these chapters, as well. Scout compares the ominous feeling in the courtroom when the jury returns to "a cold February morning, when the mockingbirds were still." Later, Atticus quietly lectures his children about the evil of white people cheating black people. In this situation, Atticus sees the African-American community as a flock of mockingbirds who are only trying to make their way in a world that is often hostile.

Lee addresses the theme of prejudice on several levels in these chapters:

In the courtroom: Jem simply can't understand how the jury could convict Tom, and Atticus shocks him with the revelation that "'when it's a white man's word against a black man's, the white man always wins.'" Atticus further reveals the jury's mindset when he explains why Tom wasn't at least given a lighter sentence.

Jem is so angered by the injustice of Tom's case that he vows to somehow make a difference when he grows up. Atticus's response allows Lee a nod to the modern Civil Rights movement: "'Don't fool yourselves — it's [white treatment of blacks] all adding up and one of these days we're going to pay the bill for it.'"

In the community: Miss Stephanie is full of questions about why Scout, Jem, and Dill were sitting in the "Colored balcony." Did Atticus plant them there for sympathy? She assumes that the children wouldn't choose to sit with African Americans. Jem is upset again by the community's seeming lack of compassion for Tom until Miss Maudie counsels him that many people in the community besides her and the Finches feel differently: "'Did it ever strike you that Judge Taylor naming Atticus to defend that boy was no accident? That Judge Taylor might have had his reasons for naming him?'"

In the Finch family: Scout is astounded when Aunt Alexandra informs her that she can't invite Walter Cunningham to play at her house "'Because—he—is—trash'" and because "'Finch women aren't interested in that sort of people.'" Jem later explains the real Maycomb caste system to Scout, introducing her to the fact that prejudice exists in whites amongst themselves as much as against people of color. Importantly, Scout ultimately decides for herself that "'there's just one kind of folks. Folks.'" Equally important is Jem's suggestion that she will come to change her mind about that.

Lee also provides a unique perspective on the role of women in these chapters. Admittedly, Atticus is less concerned about women's "place" than any other character in the novel (with the possible exception of Miss Maudie). So although he's somewhat bemused by Scout's reaction to the fact that women in Alabama can't serve on a jury, he's still forced to explain, "'I guess it's to protect our frail ladies from sordid cases like Tom's.'" Curiously, Scout has to laugh when Atticus jokes that female jurors would slow down the judicial process by asking too many questions. Hearing Atticus, who doesn't have preconceived notions about the way that women should behave, say something so silly is likely one source of Scout's laughter. Still, as much as she dislikes women's role in Maycomb society, she is ultimately willing to accept it.

Unlike her brother, Aunt Alexandra is so committed to her feminine duties that she makes woolen rugs, a very hot job, in the dead of summer. The work must be done, women must do it, and comfort doesn't matter. This woman is obsessed with turning Scout into a lady. Jem finally tells Scout that Aunt Alexandra's "'not used to girls, . . . leastways not girls like you. She's tryin' to make you a lady. Can't you take up sewin' or somethin'?'" Scout's very funny answer confirms her refusal to accept societal expectations at face value. Ironically, though, when the children fear for Atticus after Bob Ewell's threats, Jem entreats Scout to throw a tantrum reasoning "it might work if [she] cried and flung a bit, being young and a girl." When that tactic gets them nowhere, Scout is again validated against using feminine wiles to achieve a goal.

Throughout the novel, Lee has been working on two levels. First, she's trying to expose the injustice in whites' treatment of blacks. Secondly, she subtly questions the ideals of Womanhood. Through Scout, Lee shows how women who don't question their assigned roles are as oppressed as African Americans. Lee is speaking as much in favor of women's liberation as she is civil rights. By posing these questions through a young girl, Lee offers hope for the future. By this point in the story, Scout is clearly not going to accept all the trappings of being a lady. Like Miss Maudie, she will create her own definition of womanhood. Curiously, readers don't meet any other little girls in the story. Perhaps if other girls feel as Scout does, the quiet oppression of women may be nearing an end.

Glossary

salt pork pork cured in salt; esp., fatty pork from the back, side, or belly of a hog.

feral savage; wild.

furtive done or acting in a stealthy manner, as if to hinder observation; surreptitious; stealthy; sneaky.

Chapters 24 through 26

Summary

Aunt Alexandra invites Scout to attend her Missionary Society meeting. Scout helps Calpurnia serve refreshments and tries to join the ladies in conversation. The women, with the exception of Miss Maudie, gently corner Scout with their questions, taking great delight in her responses. Just about the time Scout decides that she prefers the company of men, Atticus interrupts the meeting with the news that Tom Robinson has been killed in an attempted escape.

In the kitchen, Atticus asks Calpurnia to accompany him to give the news to Tom's wife, Helen. Aunt Alexandra is almost apologetic for Atticus, but Miss Maudie takes her to task, defending him. Scout rejoins the party with Aunt Alexandra and Miss Maudie, determined to act like a lady in the face of grim circumstances. Helen takes the news about Tom badly; the rest of Maycomb has mixed reactions. Bob Ewell is vocal about his glee at Tom's death, saying, "it made one down and about two more to go."

School starts again with Jem in the seventh grade and Scout in the third. Scout notices that the Radley house is still stark and depressing, but no longer as frightening as it once was. She and Jem have been through too much to be rattled by the thought of Boo Radley. At school, Scout's teacher, Miss Gates, talks with the class about Adolph Hitler and laments the persecution of the Jews. Later, Scout remembers that she overheard Miss Gates making racist remarks about African-Americans after Tom's trial. When Scout questions Jem about this dichotomy, he becomes very angry and tells Scout never to mention the trial again. Scout then goes to Atticus who provides some consolation.

Commentary

With the trial behind them, the town works to regain some sense of normalcy. Lee uses these chapters primarily to discuss Maycomb's attitudes about women and those not white, particularly in light of Tom's death.

At the Missionary Society meeting, Scout is embarrassed when the ladies laugh at her answer to their questions. She finds an ally in Miss Maudie, though, who Scout says "never laughed at me unless I meant to be funny." Miss Maudie and Calpurnia are the two women in Scout's life who never expect her to act in a particular way. Fitting for Lee's goals in telling this story, Scout better identifies with a black woman than with her biological family. These ladies are wonderful role models for Scout, yet Aunt Alexandra doesn't recognize the positive effect that they have on her niece. Ironically, Scout learns the important things about being a lady from these unlikely sources; for all her efforts to the contrary, Aunt Alexandra only supplies Scout with negative images of womanhood, images Scout flatly rejects.

Still, Scout is intrigued by this world of women. While socializing with the ladies, Scout realizes that ideal of Womanhood is much different from the reality. When she sees Aunt Alexandra thank Miss Maudie with only body language and no words, Scout realizes the complexity of this social order: "There was no doubt about it, I must soon enter this world, where on its surface fragrant ladies rocked slowly, fanned gently, and drank cool water." But in spite of the sudden lure of being with women, Scout admits that she prefers the company of men, and readers are left believing that Scout will never become "a lady" in the sense that Aunt Alexandra would most like.

Scout is amazed at how Miss Maudie and Aunt Alexandra handle the news of Tom's death. All three of them are jarred and shaken, yet they carry on with the meeting as though nothing has happened. Scout understands the importance of doing so, even though she can't explain it. But in her first true attempt to purposely evolve into a young lady, she follows Aunt Alexandra's lead and continues serving refreshments, saying "If Aunty could be a lady at a time like this, so could I."

For the first time in the story, Christianity is used as a validation of prejudice. Both Mrs. Merriweather and Mrs. Farrow use this defense. Mrs. Merriweather criticizes her maid, Sophy, for complaining, but then passes off her own judgement as a form of Christian witness. She never inquires about why Sophy is complaining, yet she feels justified in telling her not to. Mrs. Farrow's response to dealing with African Americans is even more chilling: "'We can educate 'em till we're blue in the face, we can try till we drop to make Christians out of 'em, but there's no lady safe in her bed these nights.'" The sad irony of this conversation is that neither woman can understand why Maycomb's black community is dissatisfied.

Similarly, Miss Gates leads Scout's class in a discussion of Hitler's treatment of the Jews in Europe. During the discussion, one of the students remarks that persecution of the Jews seems so unreasonable because, after all, Jews are white. Miss Gates response fairly drips with irony: "'Jews have been persecuted since the beginning of history, even driven out of their own country. It's one of the most terrible stories in history.'" Miss Gates is oblivious to the fact that African-Americans have always and continue to be persecuted in the south. She also seems unaware that early slaves were unwillingly driven from Africa, and worse, are often excluded from their own communities 90 years since the end of slavery.

The fact that Miss Gates offers no recognition of the terrible treatment that blacks in Maycomb endure is amplified by her statement outside the classroom, "'it's time somebody taught 'em [African-Americans] a lesson, they were gettin' way above themselves, an' the next thing they think they can do is marry us.'" At least this irony isn't lost on Scout, but unfortunately the vast majority of Maycomb would agree with Miss Gates.

Several of the ladies at the meeting are quick to judge and quicker to apply the label "hypocrite" to others. All the while, they're blind to their own hypocrisy—a hypocrisy so transparent that even a child can recognize it. The ladies are genuinely concerned about "'The poverty . . . the darkness . . . the immorality'" that the Mrunas in Africa suffer, yet they're oblivious to the poverty, darkness, and immorality suffered by African Americans at the hands of whites in their own community—and in many cases their own homes.

On the surface, Tom's death goes virtually unnoticed except for a short obituary in the "Colored News." However, Lee utilizes a known racist, Mr. Underwood, to characterize Tom Robinson as a mockingbird by having him write an editorial that "likened Tom's death to the senseless slaughter of songbirds by hunters and children." By purposely writing at a child's level, Mr. Underwood underscores the town's immaturity and callousness when it comes to racial issues. As Scout rereads the editorial, she suddenly comes to the full understanding that Tom's death sentence was signed as soon as "Mayella Ewell opened her mouth and screamed." Unfortunately, the majority of the town refuses to acknowledge that fact. Instead, they believe that Tom's run at escape is typical of his race, and maintain that the jury made the right decision. In a situation of oppression, the oppressors do what's necessary to maintain their power. Admitting that Tom's arrest, conviction, and death are a travesty would cause a shift in power that whites aren't willing to accept.

Jem reaches a new level of maturity in these chapters as well. He stops Scout from killing a bug because the bug isn't hurting anyone. Obviously, Tom's trial has caused Jem to rethink his stance on his relationship with all living things. Even an insect is worth saving if it's not causing any harm. Interestingly, Scout sees this new level of tolerance in Jem as a feminine characteristic when she says, "Jem was the one who was getting more like a girl every day, not I." For all his maturity, though, Jem continues to wrestle with the implications of Tom Robinson's trial, which is why he reacts so vehemently when Scout mentions the courthouse.

Glossary

charlotte a molded dessert consisting of an outer layer of strips of bread, cake, etc. and a filling as of custard or cooked fruit.

largo slow and stately: a musical tempo.

wool short, thick, curly or crispy human hair.

Mrs. Roosevelt Eleanor Roosevelt 1884-1962; U.S. writer, social activist, and delegate at UN: wife of President Franklin D. Roosevelt.

spurious not true or genuine; false; counterfeit.

Uncle Natchell cartoon mascot for a fertilizer product called Natural Chilean Nitrate of Soda; advertisements for this product were in comic book or story form.

Chapters 27 and 28

Summary

Things settle down in Maycomb, although Bob Ewell publicly blames Atticus for him losing his job. Tom Robinson's old boss, Link Deas, gives Helen a job, but Bob Ewell makes it very difficult for her to safely walk to work. Deas puts an end to that, which makes Ewell angry.

The ladies of Maycomb decide to organize a Halloween pageant in the high school auditorium this year. Scout is assigned the role of a ham. She has a great costume for the pageant, but she can't get out of her ham suit without help.

Atticus and Aunt Alexandra don't go to the pageant because they're tired, so Jem agrees to take Scout and bring her home. On the way to the pageant, Cecil Jacobs frightens Jem and Scout. The children enjoy the festivities, but Scout embarrasses herself by making a very late entrance onstage. When it's time to go home, Scout tells Jem that she would rather leave her costume on than have to face people, and they head for home with Jem guiding Scout. Jem hears something unusual and tells Scout to be very quiet. Suddenly, a scuffle occurs. Scout hears Jem scream, and then steel-like arms begin crushing her inside the costume. Someone—Scout assumes it's Jem—pulls the attacker off her. Scout calls for Jem but gets no answer other than heavy breathing. She heads toward the breath sounds, feeling for Jem. When she touches the man's stubble, she knows he isn't Jem. Scout works to reorient herself and finally sees a strange man carrying Jem to their front door. Aunt Alexandra calls for the doctor, and Atticus calls for the sheriff.

Scout fears that Jem is dead, but Aunt Alexandra tells her that he's only unconscious as she works to disentangle Scout from the chicken wire. Dr. Reynolds arrives, and after he examines Jem, Scout and Heck Tate go into Jem's room. With Atticus is the man who brought Jem home. Scout has never seen him before. Sheriff Tate then announces that he found Bob Ewell dead under the tree where Scout and Jem were attacked.

Commentary

These two chapters comprise the novel's climax. Lee sets everything up beautifully by turning the story into a mystery of sorts, using foreshadowing to provide the reader with clues to the resolution.

The foreshadowing begins when Scout says that three things of interest happened during the fall that "did not directly concern us—the Finches—but in a way they did." All three events involve Bob Ewell, who is still very upset by the aftermath of the trial. He loses another job, and he tries to break into Judge Taylor's house. Ewell also makes it nearly impossible for Helen Robinson to get to work. The acts of revenge toward the judge and Helen hint that Ewell is serious about his earlier threats to get even with Atticus.

Ewell is angry because as Atticus puts it, "'He thought he'd be a hero, but all he got for his pain was . . . okay, we'll convict this Negro, but get back to your dump.'" In an odd way, Ewell was trying to use the circumstances of the trial to better his family's station in the community. Unfortunately, the community didn't believe his story. He loses a public job because of laziness, and realizes that he's been proven a liar and made to look a fool. Then, to add insult to injury, he believes that Link Deas is accusing him of having a romantic interest in Tom's widow, Helen. In his mind, his bitterness is completely justified and just as he felt he had to fight for his daughter's "virtue," he now has to do something to salvage his pride.

As Scout and Jem prepare to leave for the school pageant, Aunt Alexandra feels a sudden sense of foreboding, but she ignores the "pinprick of apprehension." On the way to the high school, Scout trips on the root of a large tree near the Radley house, just as she will when the two of them are attacked. Similarly, Cecil Jacobs jumps from behind a tree to scare them much the way Bob Ewell will jump from behind to make an attempt on their lives. Also on the way to school, Jem notes that Boo Radley doesn't appear to be at home, which is important given that he ultimately saves Jem and Scout's lives. Later, as the Finch children head for home, they refuse the offer for a ride and are told to be careful.

Lee also uses foreshadowing to insinuate that Boo Radley may be as much a mockingbird as Tom Robinson by having the children note that "in the darkness a solitary mocker poured out his repertoire in blissful unawareness" near the Radley house. The solitary figure of Boo Radley will save both children from death.

The issue of femininity plays its most minor role in these chapters. In fact, readers see through Scout that social conventions are in many ways unimportant. Without her costume, Scout needs something to wear and humorously notes that "in her distraction, Aunty brought me my overalls . . . handing me the garments she most despised."

Because of Jem's injuries, he won't speak for the rest of the story, making it important to note the change in Jem from the beginning of the story to this point. He began as a ten-year-old boy intent on flushing Boo Radley from his home. By the end of the novel, he is a strong, level-headed young man who "was becoming almost as good as Atticus at making you feel right when things went wrong." He puts his sister at risk when he and Dill try to peek into the Radley's house, but this night he risks his life for her. The novel begins with the events leading up to this moment, and Jem emerges as a mature adolescent well on his way to being a fine, respectable man, just like his father.

Glossary

National Recovery Act one of the measures by which President Franklin D. Roosevelt sought to assist the nation's economic recovery during the Great Depression. The act authorized an expenditure of $3.3 billion for an expansion of public works.

Cotton Tom Heflin J. Thomas "Cotton Tom" Heflin was Secretary of the State of Alabama, a member of Congress from 1905 until 1920, and a U.S. senator from 1921 until 1931.

Ladies' Law law from the criminal code of Alabama prohibiting the use of "abusive, insulting, or obscene language," especially around girls or women; punishable by up to $200 in fines, imprisonment in the county jail, or up to six months hard labor.

divinity a soft, creamy kind of candy.

climber [Informal] a person who tries to advance socially or in business.

Chapters 29 through 31

Summary

At the sheriff's request, Scout recounts what happened, realizing that one of the strange noises she heard was Jem's arm breaking. The sheriff notices knife marks on Scout's costume, and she understands that Bob Ewell had intended to kill her and Jem. She also recognizes that the stranger—the man who pulled Ewell off of her and saved both children's lives—is Boo Radley.

Scout, Atticus, Heck Tate, and Boo retire to the front porch. Atticus begins defending Jem, insisting that killing Bob Ewell was clearly self-defense. Sheriff Tate corrects Atticus, saying that Bob Ewell fell on his own knife. Atticus appreciates what Heck is trying to do, but he doesn't want anyone to cover for Jem. The sheriff remains adamant, saying that he isn't protecting Jem. As the men argue, Atticus realizes that Boo Radley killed Ewell, and it is Boo who Tate is trying to protect. They finally agree that Ewell did fall on his own knife, a decision Scout fully understands.

Boo sees Jem one more time and then asks Scout to take him home. Scout allows him to escort her to his door. She returns to Jem's room and Atticus reads aloud to her until she falls asleep. He tucks her in her own bed, and then retreats to Jem's room, where he spends the night.

Commentary

Lee uses these chapters to provide an exquisite ending to a powerful novel by allowing circumstances to come full circle. Scout finally attains her childish wish to see Boo Radley in person just one time. To her surprise, he is a nice, gentle man who appears to be somewhat sickly—not at all the monster of her imagination.

Scout realizes, too, that she, Jem, and Dill affected much of the same sorts of prejudices on Boo that Maycomb did on Tom Robinson. When she recognizes him, Scout sees that he couldn't possibly be capable of the rampant rumors she's always heard. And she's able to understand on a new level how some of Maycomb's residents feel about those who are on the fringes of society. Heck Tate hoped that Atticus could free

Tom; he's going to make sure that Arthur Radley is not put in the same situation: "'To my way of thinkin', Mr. Finch, taking the one man who's done you and this town a great service an' draggin' him . . . into the limelight . . . [is] a sin, and I'm not about to have it on my head.'"

For the endless hours Atticus has devoted to teaching Jem and Scout about human nature, compassion, and responsibility, it is Scout who has to remind him that charging Boo Radley with murder would "'be sort of like shootin' a mockingbird.'" The lessons Atticus has most hoped to teach his children are given back to him with that statement.

At the beginning of the novel, Atticus engages Scout in a white lie about their reading together to keep her in school without unduly embarrassing Miss Caroline. Here, this lesson comes full circle when Scout reminds Atticus that the white lie about Ewell keeps the town safe without jeopardizing Boo Radley.

For all of Scout's resistance to "being a lady," she instinctively acts in the most ladylike way possible when Boo asks her to take him home: "I would lead him through our house, but I would never lead him home." She insists that Boo escort her so that he won't lose face with the likes of Miss Stephanie Crawford—or any other neighbor for that matter.

Scout's maturity here is astounding for a child her age. By upholding societal conventions in this instance, she's able to protect another's—a man's—pride and standing in the community. Scout may not like or agree with society's expectations of her, but she now understands that acting within those parameters is often a show of kindness and compassion.

Significantly, inside her home, Scout leads Boo; outside, she allows him to lead her. Scout recognizes that she can project a ladylike appearance on the outside while remaining true to herself and her own convictions on the inside.

The story ends with Scout well on her way to growing up, as well. She now has some idea of what being a lady involves, and she no longer seems to mind so much. But importantly, Lee leaves readers with the remembrance that Scout the narrator is still a little girl. For all she's been through, she still feels best sitting on Atticus' lap, having him read her to sleep.

Glossary

honed it down sharpened it.

CHARACTER ANALYSES

The following critical analyses delve into the physical, emotional, and psychological traits of the literary work's major characters so that you might better understand what motivates these characters. The writer of this study guide provides this scholarship as an educational tool by which you may compare your own interpretations of the characters. Before reading the character analyses that follow, consider first writing your own short essays on the characters as an exercise by which you can test your understanding of the original literary work. Then, compare your essays to those that follow, noting discrepancies between the two. If your essays appear lacking, that might indicate that you need to re-read the original literary work or re-familiarize yourself with the major characters.

Scout (Jean Louise) Finch

That the young narrator of *To Kill a Mockingbird* goes by the nickname "Scout" is very appropriate. In the story, Scout functions as both questioner and observer. Scout asks tough questions, certainly questions that aren't "politically correct," but she can ask these questions because she is a child. As a child, Scout doesn't understand the full implication of the things happening around her, making her an objective observer and a reporter in the truest sense.

The reader should keep in mind, though, that *To Kill a Mockingbird* really presents two Scouts: the little girl experiencing the story and the adult Jean Louise who tells the story. The woman relating the story obviously recognizes that her father is exceptional. However, the child Scout complains "Our father didn't do anything . . . he never went hunting, he did not play poker or fish or drink or smoke. He sat in the living room and read." The child Scout marvels that her father knew she was listening to his conversation with Uncle Jack; the adult Jean Louise marvels that he wanted her to overhear the conversation.

Although the story takes place over the course of three years, Scout learns a lifetime's worth of lessons in that span. Here, too, the reader should remember that in many ways *To Kill a Mockingbird* is Scout's memoir—the adult Jean Louise can better understand the impact of various events than the child living through them.

Scout hates school because in many ways it actually inhibits her learning. Her teacher is appalled that she already knows how to read, instead of celebrating that fact. She is bored waiting for the rest of the class to catch up to her skill level, and she doesn't have more than a passing respect for either of the teachers she describes in the story. The most sympathy she can muster toward a frazzled Miss Caroline is to remark "Had her conduct been more friendly toward me, I would have felt sorry for her." And she is offended by Miss Gates' comments about African Americans after her staunch and moving support for the Jew's in Hitler's Europe. As a sign of her maturity, though, at the end of the story she realizes that she doesn't have much more to learn "except possibly algebra" and for that she needs the classroom.

Scout faces so many issues in the duration of the novel, but one of the most lingering for her is the question of what it means to "be a lady." Scout is a tomboy. Sometimes her brother criticizes her for "acting like a girl," other times he complains that she's not girlish enough. Dill wants to marry her, but that doesn't mean he wants to spend time with her.

Many of the boys at school are intimidated by her physical strength, yet she is told she must learn to handle herself in a ladylike way. Oddly enough, the women in her life impose more rigid requirements on her than the men do. Scout's tomboyishness drives Aunt Alexandra to distraction; Miss Caroline sees Scout's outspokenness and honesty as impertinence. Ironically, the person she most wants to please—Atticus—is least concerned about her acting in a certain way. In fact she tells Jem, "'I asked him [Atticus] if I was a problem and he said not much of one, at most one he could always figure out, and not to worry my head a second about botherin' him.'" In the end, though, when she explains why the sheriff can't charge Boo with Bob Ewell's murder, she's become the kind of person who makes her father very, very proud.

The other lesson that Scout is truly able to incorporate into her worldview is the necessity of walking in someone else's shoes. Atticus begins teaching her the importance of looking at things from the other person's point of view very early in the story. He points out her own failings in this area and demonstrates his point in his own interactions with other people. At the end of the story, Scout can put herself in Boo Radley's shoes, the person she's feared most throughout the story.

Atticus Finch

Atticus represents morality and reason in *To Kill a Mockingbird*. As a character, Atticus is even-handed throughout the story. He is one of the very few characters who never has to rethink his position on an issue.

His parenting style is quite unique in that he treats his children as adults, honestly answering any question they have. He uses all these instances as an opportunity to pass his values on to Scout and Jem. Scout says that "'Do you really think so?'. . . was Atticus' dangerous question" because he delighted in helping people see a situation in a new light. Atticus uses this approach not only with his children, but with all of Maycomb. And yet, for all of his mature treatment of Jem and Scout, he patiently recognizes that they are children and that they will make childish mistakes and assumptions. Ironically, Atticus' one insecurity seems to be in the child-rearing department, and he often defends his ideas about raising children to those more experienced and more traditional.

His stern but fair attitude toward Jem and Scout reaches into the courtroom as well. He politely proves that Bob Ewell is a liar; he respectfully questions Mayella about her role in Tom's crisis. One of the things that his longtime friend Miss Maudie admires about him is that "'Atticus Finch is the same in his house as he is on the public streets.'" The only time he seriously lectures his children is on the evils of taking advantage of those less fortunate or less educated, a philosophy he carries into the animal world by his refusal to hunt. And although most of the town readily pins the label "trash" on other people, Atticus reserves that distinction for those people who unfairly exploit others.

Atticus believes in justice and the justice system. He doesn't like criminal law, yet he accepts the appointment to Tom Robinson's case. He knows before he begins that he's going to lose this case, but that doesn't stop him from giving Tom the strongest defense he possibly can. And, importantly, Atticus doesn't put so much effort into Tom's case because he's an African American, but because he is innocent. Atticus feels that the justice system should be color blind, and he defends Tom as an innocent man, not a man of color.

Atticus is the adult character least infected by prejudice in the novel. He has no problem with his children attending Calpurnia's church, or with a black woman essentially raising his children. He admonishes Scout not to use racial slurs, and is careful to always use the terms acceptable for his time and culture. He goes to Helen's home to tell her of Tom's death, which means a white man spending time in the black community. Other men in town would've sent a messenger and left it at that. His lack of prejudice doesn't apply only to other races, however. He is unaffected by Mrs. Dubose's caustic tongue, Miss Stephanie Crawford's catty gossip, and even Walter Cunningham's thinly veiled threat on his life. He doesn't retaliate when Bob Ewell spits in his face because he understands that he has wounded Ewell's pride—the only real possession this man has. Atticus accepts these people because he is an expert at "climb[ing] into [other people's] skin and walk[ing] around in it."

Jem Finch

Jem ages from 10 to 13 over the course of *To Kill a Mockingbird*, a period of great change in any child's life. Jem is no exception to this rule. Interestingly, the changes he undergoes are seen from the point-of-view of a younger sister, which gives a unique perspective on his growth.

Jem represents the idea of bravery in the novel, and the way that his definition changes over the course of the story is important. The shift that occurs probably has as much to do with age as experience, although the experiences provide a better framework for the reader. When the story begins, Jem's idea of bravery is simply touching the side of the Radley house and then only because "In all his life, Jem had never declined a dare." But as the story progresses, Jem learns about bravery from Atticus facing a mad dog, from Mrs. Dubose's fight with addiction, and from Scout's confrontation with the mob at the jail, among others. And along the way, he grows from a boy who drags his sister along as a co-conspirator to a young gentleman who protects his Scout and tries to help her understand the implications of the events around her.

His own sister finds Jem a genuinely likeable boy, if sometimes capable of "maddening superiority." He very much wants to be like his father, and plans to follow him into law. He idolizes Atticus and would rather risk personal injury than disappoint his father. As he grows older, he begins to do what is right even though his decision may not be popular. For instance, when Dill sneaks into Scout's bedroom after running away from home, Jem can only say, "'You oughta let your mother know where you are'" and makes the difficult decision to involve Atticus. Afterward, he's temporarily exiled by his friends, but he maintains the rightness of his decision without apology.

Like many adolescents, Jem is idealistic. Even after Atticus' long explanation about the intricacies of the Tom Robinson case, Jem is unable to accept the jury's conviction. In fact, he is ready to overhaul the justice system and abolish juries all together. Wisely, Atticus doesn't try to squelch or minimize Jem's feelings; by respecting his son, Atticus allows Jem to better cope with the tragedy. Still, Jem turns on Scout when she tells him about Miss Gates' racist remarks at the courthouse, shouting, "'I never wanta hear about that courthouse again, ever, ever, you hear me?'" His coping skills are still developing, and his family is the one group that gives him the room that he needs to hone them.

Ironically, Jem, who so strongly identifies with Tom Robinson, is the only person in the story who is left with physical evidence of the whole event. More ironic still is the fact that Jem's injury leaves "His left arm . . . somewhat shorter than the right" just like Tom Robinson's, and Tom Robinson sustained his injury at approximately the same age. That the man responsible for breaking Jem's arm was also responsible for sending Tom to prison (and indirectly, responsible for his death) serves to drive the irony home.

The adult Jean Louise doesn't provide much insight into the adult Jeremy Atticus Finch, but from the fact that the story begins with their disagreement over when various events started, the reader can assume that they maintained a similar relationship into adulthood.

Dill Harris

Because he hails from Mississippi, Dill Harris is an outsider, but having relatives in Maycomb, as well as being a child, grants him immediate acceptance in the town. Dill is an interesting character because his personality is a compilation of many of the story's other characters. As such, Dill functions as a sort of moral thermometer for the reader in understanding Maycomb. Readers, especially those who don't live in the South, are as much strangers to Maycomb as Dill is, and so he paves the way for the reader's objective observance of the story Scout has to tell.

Dill is an observer much like Scout; however, he has no vested interest or innate understanding of the various folks he encounters. Dill doesn't know his biological father, just as Scout doesn't know her mother. In his attempts to lure Boo Radley outside, Dill's not much different than Bob Ewell with Tom Robinson, although admittedly, Dill's intentions are nowhere near as heinous. He tells enormous lies and concocts unlikely stories just as Mayella does during Tom's trial. He often pretends to be something he isn't, just like Dolphus Raymond does when he comes into town. He risks his safety to run away to Maycomb just as Jem risks his when he goes to collect his pants from the Radleys.

Dill's fantastic stories bring the question of lying to the forefront of *To Kill a Mockingbird*. Dill's lies incense Scout, but she learns that "one must lie under certain circumstances and at all times when one can't do anything about them," a statement that foreshadows Mayella's predicament. Ironically, Dill, who so easily lies, sobs when the Ewell's succeed in the lies they tell about Tom Robinson.

Boo Radley and Tom Robinson

Boo Radley and Tom Robinson share many similarities in spite of fact that one man is white and the other black. By juxtaposing these two characters, Lee proves that justice and compassion reach beyond the boundary of color and human prejudices. The novel's title is a metaphor for both men, each of whom is a mockingbird. In this case however, one mockingbird is shot, the other is forced to kill.

Boo and Tom are handicapped men. She hints that Boo may be physically unhealthy, and she makes statements that lead the reader to believe he may be mentally unstable. However, no character sheds any light on his actual condition, leaving the reader wondering whether Boo's family protects him or further handicaps him. Tom is physically handicapped, like a bird with a broken wing, but his race is probably a bigger "disability" in the Maycomb community. As a result of these handicaps, both men's lives are cut short. Whatever Boo's problems may be, the reader knows that something happened to Boo that has caused him to become a recluse. For all practical purposes, Tom's life ends when a white woman decides to accuse him of rape.

Boo sees Scout and Jem as his children, which is why he parts with things that are precious to him, why he mends Jem's pants and covers Scout with a blanket, and why he ultimately kills for them: "Boo's children needed him." Apparently his family disapproves of his affection for the children or Mr. Radley wouldn't have cemented the knothole. But Boo is undeterred and loves them, even with the probable knowledge that he is the object of their cruel, childish games. Tom also recognizes Mayella as a person in need. On the witness stand, he testifies that he gladly helped her because "'Mr. Ewell didn't seem to help her none, and neither did the chillun.'" Tom helps Mayella at great personal expense.

Both men know their town very well. Unbeknownst to the Finch children, Boo has watched them grow up. The reader can fairly assume that Boo is also familiar with the Ewells, and probably doesn't think much more of them than the rest of Maycomb. Boo and Tom have had minor skirmishes with the law, but that past doesn't tarnish the kindness they show to others in the story. The moment that Mayella makes a pass at Tom, he inherently knows that he's in serious danger. Truthfully, he probably knew that helping her without pay was not the safest thing for him to do, but the compassion of one human being for another won out over societal expectations.

The children treat Boo with as much prejudice as the town shows Tom Robinson. They assign characteristics to Boo without validation; they want to see Boo, not as their neighbor, but as a carnival-freak-show-type curiosity. Ironically, watching the injustice that Tom suffers helps the children understand why Boo may choose to be a recluse: "'it's because he *wants* to stay inside.'"

Aunt Alexandra and Miss Maudie Atkinson

Aunt Alexandra and Miss Maudie are roughly the same age and grew up as neighbors at Finch's Landing. But for all the background these women share, they couldn't be more opposite. Lee uses the contrasts between these two characters to further delineate the theme of tolerance in *To Kill a Mockingbird*.

Aunt Alexandra is very conscious of Maycomb's social mores, chooses to live within its constrictions, and "given the slightest chance she would exercise her royal prerogative: she would arrange, advise, caution, and warn." Even her clothing is tight and restrictive. Miss Maudie, on the other hand, sets herself towards the outside of Maycomb's conventionality. Like Atticus, she stays within bounds, but follows her own code.

Although Miss Maudie is quick to welcome Aunt Alexandra as her new neighbor, she's also quick to take her to task. When Aunt Alexandra states, "'I can't say I approve of everything he does, Maudie, but he's my brother,'" Miss Maudie reminds her that Atticus is doing a wonderful thing and that many in the town support him, even if that support is quiet. Aunt Alexandra is also extremely critical of Atticus's parenting style, while Miss Maudie is much more sympathetic. But then, Miss Maudie has a delightful sense of humor, a trait Aunt Alexandra does not possess.

Aunt Alexandra works hard at being feminine, but Miss Maudie doesn't seem to care about those things. She wears men's overalls when she works in the garden, but is equally comfortable in more traditional garb. Aunt Alexandra has a personal quest to make Scout "behave like a sunbeam," but Miss Maudie accepts her as she is. Consequently, Scout finds in Miss Maudie a kindred spirit who helps her make sense of being female and, with Atticus, helps Scout develop tolerance. Miss Maudie treats the children in an adult manner, much like Atticus does. She never laughs at Scout's mistakes and she trusts the children to play in her yard within the boundaries she's set for them. Aunt Alexandra is "analogous to Mount Everest: . . . cold and there" while Miss Maudie is warm enough to pop out her dentures for Scout to see.

Miss Maudie has a quiet spirituality that shows itself only when taunted by "'the foot-washers [who] think women are a sin by definition.'" Aunt Alexandra displays her beliefs much more publicly. She's active in the Missionary Society, which appears to be as much a social club as a religious organization. Tolerance isn't a big part of the Missionary Society meetings, either. The ladies' lamentations over the living conditions of the Mrunas, an African tribe, leads to a discussion about how ungrateful the women believe Maycomb's African-American community to be. Miss Maudie is the person who ends that line of conversation with two sentences. Aunt Alexandra may not always agree with the course of discussion, but she refuses to be confrontational outside of her own family.

Bob and Mayella Ewell

The Ewells know that they are the lowest of the low amongst the whites in Maycomb. They have no money, no education, and no breeding. The single thing that elevates them at any level in the community is the fact that they're white. Like most people in similar situations, Bob and Mayella would like to better their station in life. However, Bob is unwilling to put forth the effort necessary to change his family's lot and Mayella doesn't have the resources to change her own life.

With her mother dead, Mayella becomes a surrogate wife for her father and mother for her younger siblings. The fact that Mayella wants a better life for herself is evidenced by the red geraniums she grows so lovingly—they're the only sign of beauty in a dismal, filthy shack and yard. She can't attend school because she has to take care of her younger siblings, especially when her father leaves on days-long drinking binges. She's involved in an incestuous and abusive relationship, but she doesn't have anywhere to go or anyone to help her. At 19, her future is set. She will most likely stay with her family, continuing to be both sexually and physically abused, until she marries and starts the cycle anew.

The idea of having an affair with a black man is exciting in a dangerous sort of way, but more importantly, making advances toward Tom gives Mayella power. This completely powerless woman has total control over Tom in this situation. If he were to agree to a liaison with her, then he would remain at her beck and call for the rest of his life. Readers know what happened when he didn't agree. In an attempt to gain some power in a shabby, pitiful existence, Mayella costs a man his life. Ironically, when Atticus finally shows Mayella the respect she so craves, she accuses him of making fun of her and ultimately refuses to answer his questions.

Bob Ewell would also like to improve his family's station, but the fact that "he was the only man [Scout] ever heard of who was fired from the WPA for laziness" proves that he isn't willing to earn it. Ewell is a drunkard and an abuser who is despised throughout the community, and very likely by his own family. But in accusing Tom Robinson, he sees what he believes is a brass ring. In his mind, the town should think him a hero for saving Maycomb's white women from a "dangerous" black man. Defending his daughter by going to court should raise his family's stature. If they don't gain more respect from the community, at least Bob won't have to live with talk in the black community about a white woman making a play for a married black man. Unfortunately, all of Ewell's plans backfire. By the end of the trial, he and his daughter are proven liars, he's been publicly identified as a sexually and physically abusive father who fails to provide for his family, and the entire town knows that Mayella made sexual overtures toward Tom. Instead of improving his life, Ewell cements his family's horrible reputation once and for all.

In this situation, Bob Ewell can do little but try to recover his own pride. He makes good on his threats to harm the people who embarrassed him in court. He rejoices in Tom's death. Bob Ewell is the kind of person who actually seems to enjoy being despicable.

CRITICAL ESSAYS

On the pages that follow, the writer of this study guide provides critical scholarship on various aspects of Harper Lee's *To Kill a Mockingbird*. These interpretive essays are intended solely to enhance your understanding of the original literary work; they are supplemental materials and are not to replace your reading of *To Kill a Mockingbird*. When you're finished reading *To Kill a Mockingbird*, and prior to your reading this study guide's critical essays, consider making a bulleted list of what you think are the most important themes and symbols. Write a short paragraph under each bullet explaining why you think that theme or symbol is important; include at least one short quote from the original literary work that supports your contention. Then, test your list and reasons against those found in the following essays. Do you include themes and symbols that the study guide author doesn't? If so, this self test might indicate that you are well on your way to understanding original literary work. But if not, perhaps you will need to re-read *To Kill a Mockingbird*.

Racial Relations in the Southern United States

The racial concerns that Harper Lee addresses in *To Kill a Mockingbird* began long before her story starts and continued long after. In order to sift through the many layers of prejudice that Lee exposes in her novel, the reader needs to understand the complex history of race relations in the South.

Jim Crow Laws

Many states—particularly in the South—passed "Jim Crow" laws (named after a black minstrel show character), which severely limited how African Americans could participate in society. The U. S. Supreme Court paved the ways for these laws in 1883 when the court ruled that it couldn't enforce the 14th Amendment at the individual level. The first Jim Crow law appeared in 1890; the laws increased from there and lasted until the Civil Rights movement of the 1960s.

Many whites at the time believed that instead of progressing as a race, blacks were regressing with the abolition of slavery. Southern churches frequently upheld this racist thinking, which also helped give the Jim Crow laws some of their power.

Ironically, African-American churches were as likely to uphold the Jim Crow laws as white churches were. The continued oppression of one group over another is largely psychological. The dominant group first uses force to obtain their power. Slowly, the group being oppressed begins to feel hopeless that the situation can change and begins to unwittingly buy into the oppression as the norm. Before the Civil Rights movement gained momentum, many African-American churches concentrated on helping their congregations deal with the oppression rather than trying to end it.

Jim Crow laws extended into almost every facet of public life. The laws stipulated that blacks use separate entrances into public buildings, have separate restrooms and drinking fountains, and sit in the back of trains and buses. Blacks and whites were not allowed to be served food in the same room in a restaurant, play pool together, share the same prisons, or be buried in the same cemeteries. African Americans couldn't play professional sports with white teammates or serve in the armed forces with white soldiers. Black children were educated in separate schools. Black barbers couldn't wait on white female clients, and white female nurses couldn't attend to black male patients. Not every law applied in every state, but the Jim Crow laws were demoralizing and far reaching, all in the name of protecting white culture and power.

Interracial Marriage

At the time Lee wrote *To Kill a Mockingbird,* white people had control over the communities they lived in, but many members of the elite class feared that African Americans would make inroads into the white world by marrying and having children with whites. Thus, interracial marriage was outlawed in many states.

Biracial children were referred to as "mulatto," a word derived from "mule," because, like mules, these children were thought to be the offspring of an unnatural union. Ironically, biracial children born to black mothers were not seen as a threat to white superiority, so most people looked the other way when a white man—like Dolphus Raymond in the novel—chose to marry a black woman.

The fear of interracial unions reached its apex in a widely held, unrealistic fear that African American men would rape and impregnate white women as a means of penetrating white society and, worse, white power.

This sort of crime virtually never happened. However, the frenzy that characterized the "rape complex" led to drastic and deadly results: lynching became the primary means of dealing with any accusation of rape of a white woman by a black man. When the mob comes to lynch Tom Robinson at the jail, Lee alludes to the reality of black men who lived on the receiving end of this treatment.

The Scottsboro Trials

Lee may have gotten the inspiration for Tom Robinson's case from the Scottsboro Trials of 1931, which were a result of the ideals and laws discussed in the preceding sections. In the Scottsboro case, two white women accused nine black men of raping them as they traveled from Tennessee to Alabama. Both of the women, the nine black men, and two white men hopped a freight car and headed south. (During the Great Depression, jobs were scarce, and the unemployed frequently rode from place to place in empty boxcars in search of work. Although unemployment among blacks was much higher—and in spite of the Jim Crow laws—blacks and whites ultimately competed for the same jobs, a fact that whites greatly resented.)

During the train ride the two groups of men fought, and the white men were forced off the train. When the rest of the hobos arrived in Alabama, they were arrested for vagrancy. Both women were of questionable background; one was a known prostitute. They used the ideal of Southern womanhood as their "Get Out of Jail Free Card" and accused the nine African Americans of rape.

Although a doctor's examination revealed no signs of forced intercourse or any sort of struggle, eight of the nine men were sentenced to death. The Supreme Court ordered a second trial for the Scottsboro "boys," during which one of the women recanted her testimony, denying that she or the other woman had been raped. Nonetheless, the eight men were convicted a second time. The appeals process continued for several years. Some of the men escaped prison, others were paroled. The last man was released from prison in 1950; one of the men received a pardon in 1976.

Because of deep-rooted anti-black sentiment, two white women with skeletons in their own closets were able to deprive eight men of several years of their lives.

The Civil Rights Movement

The black community had shown spurts of enthusiasm in pursuing Civil Rights since the end of slavery. By the 1950s, however, the latest interest in the Civil Rights movement had lost a good deal of steam. Many African Americans seemed resigned to accepting the Jim Crow laws and living within the existing system. Educated blacks in Alabama were looking for something to rekindle the interest in Civil Rights amongst the black community. They found that "something" in a woman named Rosa Parks.

On a December day in 1955, Parks boarded a full Montgomery, Alabama bus, tired after a long day's work. She sat at the back of the bus's white section. When a white person boarded, the bus driver ordered Parks and several other black riders to move, and she refused. Her subsequent arrest mobilized the African-American community into a yearlong bus boycott that ultimately ended segregation on public transportation. Parks was an educated woman who was concerned about the plight of Southern blacks. Although she did not board the bus intending to take a stand, when the opportunity arose, she accepted the challenge.

When the Supreme Court overturned Alabama's segregation laws regarding public transportation, the Civil Rights movement gained momentum. Martin Luther King, Jr., a Montgomery, Alabama minister, rose as the recognized leader of the movement. Several women worked behind the scenes organizing the boycott and keeping the movement alive.

Concurrent with the Montgomery bus boycott, another Civil Rights issue came to the forefront at the University of Alabama in Tuscaloosa. There, a young black woman named Autherine Lucy enrolled in an all-white school. Because of racial tensions, the Board of Trustees expelled her from the campus after only a few months; however, the stage was set for more skirmishes with Civil Rights' issues. (Lucy received her Masters degree from the Tuscaloosa campus in 1992.)

In 1957, schools in Little Rock, Arkansas underwent desegregation. Resentment and resistance ran so high and the threat of violence was so great that federal troops were sent to maintain order.

Harper Lee wrote *To Kill a Mockingbird* in the midst of these developments. Her story was informed not only by the laws and attitudes that were part of her youth and her culture, but also by the Civil Rights movement. The Civil Rights struggle continues today at various levels, making *To Kill a Mockingbird* a timeless novel.

Comparing *To Kill a Mockingbird* to Its Movie Version

The film version of *To Kill a Mockingbird* (1962), which stars Gregory Peck as Atticus and Mary Badham as Scout, is as much a classic as the novel itself. (The film received eight Academy Awards nominations and netted awards for Best Actor, Best Screenplay Based on Material from Another Medium, and Best Art Direction—Set Decoration, Black and White.)

Ideally, a novel and its film version complement each other, which, on many levels, is the case with *To Kill a Mockingbird*. However, film can accomplish things that novels can't, and vice versa. Likewise, film has limitations that a novel doesn't. This essay explores some of the differences between *To Kill a Mockingbird*, the film and the novel.

Narration

By its nature, film is a visual medium, which makes a first-person story difficult to tell. To have Scout narrating throughout the film as she does in the book would prove distracting, so Scout as narrator is only presented to set the mood of a scene in the film. As a result, viewers don't get a strong sense of Scout's first-person narration as they do in the book; instead, they simply notice the childlike perspective portrayed in the story. (The film uses music to help reinforce the child's point of view. The music is very elementary, and much of the score is composed of single notes without chords or embellishments.)

Because the narration is not as straightforward in the film, the film seems to shift more to Jem's experiences. For example, Jem finds all the articles in the tree. Jem accompanies Atticus to tell Helen Robinson of her husband's death. Jem is left alone to watch his sister. Scout is still an important character, but the film expands on her brother's role.

Characters

A film has less time to tell its story and therefore often concentrates the events of a story into fewer characters; when a book makes the transition to film, characters and their actions are often combined. For instance, Miss Stephanie Crawford is Dill's aunt and Cecil Jacobs, not Francis Hancock, drives Scout to break her promise to Atticus about fighting. Aunt Alexandra isn't present in the movie at all, so the issue of Scout "acting like a lady" never plays a major role in the film.

Film also often introduces new characters to help develop the story line. In the film, Scout and Jem have a conversation about their deceased mother which brings her alive for the viewers; the book devotes a single paragraph to her. Viewers also meet Tom Robinson's children and father. His father isn't mentioned in the book, and his children receive only a brief mention.

The benefit of film is that viewers get to see the characters. They can put a face with a name, so to speak. And characters can say things with facial expressions, hand gestures, and posture that an author must describe to readers. Many people enjoy the advantage of being able to visualize a character; however, viewers can be thrown out of the story if the actor playing the part doesn't fit the reader's vision of the character. For instance, the actress who plays Miss Maudie is thin, much younger, and more conventional than Scout describes in the book, which takes some of the bite out of the character. On the other hand, Gregory Peck, by Lee's own assertion, is the perfect embodiment of Atticus Finch, which gives the character a far greater depth than the book, alone, can provide.

Focus

Because a film has a limited time in which to tell the story, events from a novel are invariably dropped when the book becomes a film. Although the film version of *To Kill a Mockingbird* includes every major event from the novel, the screenplay takes place over two years, not three, and many events are left out. For example, the children have virtually no contact with Mrs. Dubose, and the film never shows the inside of a classroom, so viewers don't experience any of the episodes with Miss Caroline, Miss Gates, and some of the other minor characters that create Maycomb's texture and layers.

Lee's novel is a coming-of-age story influenced by a major event in the community and within one family. Scout not only tries to understand and process the trial, but she's also wrestling with the expectations those around her have of little girls. The film, on the other hand, is a courtroom drama that happens to include something about the lead attorney's home life. In its film version, *To Kill a Mockingbird* only touches on the issues of femininity. The movie never gets into Maycomb's caste system, so viewers don't necessarily know that the Ewells are considered to be "trash."

The implied incest between Bob and Mayella Ewell is never discussed during the course of the trial. Unlike today's films, movies in 1962 weren't allowed to cover such controversial subject matter. Instead, films had to find ways to work around taboo subjects. In this case, the film works around the incest issue by showing Bob Ewell's unscrupulous behavior in other ways. For instance, he begins stalking Jem and Scout before Tom's trial begins, and viewers can see from Mayella's facial expressions in the courtroom that she's frightened of her father.

The courtroom scenes are condensed in the film. Gregory Peck as Atticus Finch delivers a shortened version of Atticus's closing arguments to the jury. The lines he does say are verbatim, but several points from the speech aren't included. Neither does the film explore the aftermath of the trial or portray the conversations Atticus has with his children in trying to help them understand the situation.

The film addresses the plight of African Americans only through the trial. Calpurnia is treated respectfully by everyone, the children never attend Calpurnia's church, and on the day of the trial, blacks and whites enter the courtroom together (although the blacks, and Scout, Jem, and Dill, sit separately in a balcony, just as they do in the book). Remember, though, that at the time this film was in theaters, audiences wouldn't have needed an explanation for these sorts of things. They knew first-hand the challenges African Americans faced. The idea that blacks would sit separate from whites would have been expected—or understood, at the very least—by anyone viewing the film.

Film is very much reflective of the original audience's culture. As a film ages, audiences need more information to fully grasp the story. The fact that the film version of *To Kill a Mockingbird* is still so powerful is a testament to a fine adaptation of a classic story.

CLIFFSNOTES REVIEW

Use this CliffsNotes Review to test your understanding of the original text, and reinforce what you've learned in this book. After you work through the review and essay questions, identify the quote, and complete the fun and useful practice projects, you're well on your way to understanding a comprehensive and meaningful interpretation of *To Kill a Mockingbird*.

Q&A

Answer the following questions to further your understanding of the story:

1. _____ feels sorry for the plight of the Jews in Germany but not for the African-Americans at home.

2. Who taught Calpurnia to read and write?

a. Atticus

b. Miss Maudie's aunt

c. Reverend Skyes

3. What does Scout's cousin, Francis Hancock, call Atticus?

a. A liar

b. A coward

c. A "nigger-lover"

4. _____ tells Jem he cemented the knothole because the tree in his yard is dying.

Answers: (1) Miss Gates. (2) b. (3) c. (4) Nathan Radley.

Identify the Quote: Find Each Quote in *To Kill a Mockingbird*

Identify which character said the following, and explain the context in which it was said:

1. " . . . before I can live with other folks I've got to live with myself. The one thing that doesn't abide by majority rule is a person's conscience."

2. "I can use one hand as good as the other. One hand as good as the other."

3. "Alec, shut the doors. Nobody leaves here till we have ten dollars."

4. "We're the safest folks in the world."

5. Hey, Mr. Cunningham. How's your entailment gettin' along?"

Answers: (1) [When Jem goes to apologize to Mrs. Dubose for destroying her flowers, Atticus explains to Scout why he's made the unpopular decision to defend Tom Robinson.] (2) [During his testimony, Bob Ewell demonstrates that he is left-handed, but shows his lack of education when his lawyer asks him whether he's ambidextrous.] (3) [Reverend Skyes is taking up a collection for Tom Robinson's family, who are members of the church. Scout and Jem are surprised at his heavy-handed tactics.] (4) [Miss Maudie's response to Jem's assertion that he used to think the people in Maycomb were the best in the world.] (5) [As Scout attempts to ease the tension between Atticus and the mob in front of the jail, she spots one of Atticus' clients, who is also the father of one of her classmates.]

Essay Questions

Following are essay questions for you to answer:

1. Why does Atticus choose not to reveal to his children that Judge Taylor appointed him to Tom's case? How does his decision affect Scout's perception of her father?

2. Do you think that the adult Jean Louise telling the story through Scout's eyes may have added any embellishments to the story? Think of an event from your own life that occurred at least five years ago. Do you see the event differently now? How does memory and education affect your perception of the event?

3. Read *Snow Falling on Cedars* by David Guterson. How are the stories alike? How are they different? Compare Atticus Finch and Tom Robinson with Nels Gudmundsson and Kabuo Miyamoto. Compare Scout's and Hatsue's understanding of their place in their communities.

4. If Scout and Jem's mother were still alive, how might the following people be different: Atticus, Scout, Jem, Calpurnia, and Aunt Alexandra?

5. Would Heck Tate have filed charges against Tom Robinson so quickly if Tom were white? Why or why not? Would Sheriff Tate have been so unwilling to file charges against Boo Radley if Boo was black? Why or why not?

6. Read the play *To Kill a Mockingbird*, by Christopher Sergel. What elements in the story are different? What limitations does the book have that the stage doesn't? What limitations does the stage have that the book doesn't? Does Sergel tell the same story that Harper Lee does? What events does Sergel highlight as important? Why do you think he made those choices? Do you agree with his choices?

7. Compare and contrast the relationship between Jem and Scout with the relationship between Atticus and Aunt Alexandra.

8. Based on what you know about Scout, describe the adult Jean Louise Finch.

9. Suppose that Mayella had admitted that she was lying when she testified against Tom. What would have happened to her? What would've happened to Tom? How would Scout, Jem, and Dill perceive the situation differently? Would the town have been willing to accept Tom's innocence? Why or why not?

10. What significance do the items that Boo leaves for the children have? What do they tell you about Boo? Why does his brother object so strongly to his leaving items for the children?

11. Read Truman Capote's *Other Voices, Other Rooms*. Capote based the character of Idabel on Harper Lee, his childhood friend, just as she based the character of Dill on him. Compare Idabel and Scout. Do the two characterizations give you any insight to Harper Lee? How are the characters different from each other? Compare Joel and Idabel's relationship to Dill and Scout's. What role does friendship play in each of these stories? Compare and contrast the setting in the two stories.

12. Harper Lee uses language and grammar that mirrors how the characters actually speak. Is this technique helpful in understanding the characters? Is it distracting? Could Lee have told the same story with the same impact if she'd used proper grammar throughout?

13. Read Mark Twain's *Huckleberry Finn*. Compare the lessons Scout learns with those that Huck learns. How is Jim like or unlike Tom Robinson? *To Kill a Mockingbird* and *Huckleberry Finn* are both novels that have undergone many censorship attempts, especially in schools and public libraries. Why do you think people would want to censor these stories? Is censorship ever appropriate? Why or why not?

14. Compare the way Miss Caroline treats Scout on her first day of school with the way the town treats Mayella Ewell.

15. What, if any, prejudices do African Americans face in today's world? Have the issues that Lee discusses in *To Kill a Mockingbird* been resolved or are they ongoing? What forms of prejudice can you identify in your own community? Have you ever been the victim of prejudice? Did the situation end justly? Explain.

16. Why does Boo Radley stay inside all the time?

Projects

Following are some projects to further your understanding of *To Kill a Mockingbird*:

1. Assume the role of one of the following characters: Aunt Alexandra, Miss Stephanie Crawford, Mrs. Grace Merriweather, Miss Gates, Calpurnia, Helen Robinson, Dill, Mr. Gilmer, Walter Cunningham, Dolphus Raymond, Reverend Skyes, or Mr. Underwood. Tell Tom's story from that character's perspective, and then deliver a speech, in character, to defend or accuse Tom of raping Mayella.

2. Search the Web for information about the Civil Rights movement. Choose one person involved in the movement with whom you're not already familiar and present an oral biography of that person based on your Internet research.

3. Create a collage that represents some aspect of the Civil Rights movement.

4. Based on the information in *To Kill a Mockingbird*, draw a picture of Boo Radley.

5. Select a song that represents one of the themes in *To Kill a Mockingbird*. Play the song for your class and discuss your choice and the theme it represents.

CLIFFSNOTES RESOURCE CENTER

Just because you finish reading *To Kill a Mockingbird*, doesn't mean that you need to stop learning about the events and issues that inform this novel. This Resource Center offers you other books and Internet sites to explore. What's more, we've put all kinds of pertinent information at www.cliffsnotes.com. Look for these resources at your favorite bookstore or local library and on the Internet. When you're online, make your first stop www.cliffsnotes.com where you'll find more incredibly useful information about Lee's *To Kill a Mockingbird*.

Books

This CliffsNotes book, published by Hungry Minds, Inc., provides a meaningful interpretation of Lee's *To Kill a Mockingbird*. If you're looking for information about the author and related works, check out these other publications:

Modern Critical Interpretations: To Kill a Mockingbird, edited by Harold Bloom, offers a series of essays by different authors on various aspects of the novel and film. Philadelphia: Chelsea House Publishers, 1999.

Other Voices, Other Rooms, by Truman Capote, is another story that takes place in the South. Lee and Capote were childhood friends. She based the character of Dill on Capote; he based the character of Idabel on Lee. New York: Random House, 1948.

Understanding To Kill a Mockingbird, by Claudia Durst Johnson, provides an explanation of the issues surrounding the novel, complete with supporting historical documents. Johnson is a retired University of Alabama professor and an expert on Lee's book. Greenwood Press, 1994.

To Kill a Mockingbird: A Full-Length Play, by Christopher Sergel, is an adaption of Lee's novel for the stage. The Dramatic Publishing Company, 1970.

It's easy to find books published by Wiley Publishing, Inc. You'll find them in your favorite bookstores and on the Internet. We also have three Web sites that you can use to read about all the books we publish:

- `www.cliffsnotes.com`
- `www.dummies.com`
- `www.wiley.com`

Internet

Check out these Web sites for more information about Harper Lee and *To Kill a Mockingbird*.

To Kill a Mockingbird: The Student Survival Guide— `www.lausd.k12.ca.us/Belmont_HS/tkm/`—offers over 400 definitions and explanations for colloquialisms and allusions in the novel.

To Kill a Mockingbird: Growing up in the 1930s— `www.slc.k12.ut.us/webweavers/jillc/mbird.html`—a fun and thought provoking site that gives readers an excellent understanding of life in the Southern United States during the 1930s. The Web page also includes exercises to help students put this new understanding to use.

Send Us Your Favorite Tips

In your quest for knowledge, have you ever experienced that sublime moment when you figure out a trick that saves time or trouble? If you've discovered a useful tip that helped you understand Lee's *To Kill a Mockingbird* more effectively and you'd like to share it, the CliffsNotes staff would love to hear from you. Go to our Web site at `www.cliffsnotes.com` and click the Talk to Us button. If we select your tip, we may publish it as part of CliffsNotes Daily, our exciting, free e-mail newsletter. To find out more or to subscribe to a newsletter, go to `www.cliffsnotes.com` on the Web.

Index

NOTES

NOTES

NOTES

NOTES

NOTES

CliffsNotes

CliffsNotes

LITERATURE NOTES

Absalom, Absalom!
The Aeneid
Agamemnon
Alice in Wonderland
All the King's Men
All the Pretty Horses
All Quiet on the
    Western Front
All's Well &
    Merry Wives
American Poets of the
    20th Century
American Tragedy
Animal Farm
Anna Karenina
Anthem
Antony and Cleopatra
Aristotle's Ethics
As I Lay Dying
The Assistant
As You Like It
Atlas Shrugged
Autobiography of
    Ben Franklin
Autobiography of
    Malcolm X
The Awakening
Babbit
Bartleby & Benito
    Cereno
The Bean Trees
The Bear
The Bell Jar
Beloved
Beowulf
The Bible
Billy Budd & Typee
Black Boy
Black Like Me
Bleak House
Bless Me, Ultima
The Bluest Eye & Sula
Brave New World
The Brothers Karamazov

The Call of the Wild &
    White Fang
Candide
The Canterbury Tales
Catch-22
Catcher in the Rye
The Chosen
The Color Purple
Comedy of Errors…
Connecticut Yankee
The Contender
The Count of
    Monte Cristo
Crime and Punishment
The Crucible
Cry, the Beloved
    Country
Cyrano de Bergerac
Daisy Miller &
    Turn…Screw
David Copperfield
Death of a Salesman
The Deerslayer
Diary of Anne Frank
Divine Comedy-I.
    Inferno
Divine Comedy-II.
    Purgatorio
Divine Comedy-III.
    Paradiso
Doctor Faustus
Dr. Jekyll and Mr. Hyde
Don Juan
Don Quixote
Dracula
Electra & Medea
Emerson's Essays
Emily Dickinson Poems
Emma
Ethan Frome
The Faerie Queene
Fahrenheit 451
Far from the Madding
    Crowd
A Farewell to Arms
Farewell to Manzanar
Fathers and Sons
Faulkner's Short Stories

Faust Pt. I & Pt. II
The Federalist
Flowers for Algernon
For Whom the Bell Tolls
The Fountainhead
Frankenstein
The French
    Lieutenant's Woman
The Giver
Glass Menagerie &
    Streetcar
Go Down, Moses
The Good Earth
The Grapes of Wrath
Great Expectations
The Great Gatsby
Greek Classics
Gulliver's Travels
Hamlet
The Handmaid's Tale
Hard Times
Heart of Darkness &
    Secret Sharer
Hemingway's
    Short Stories
Henry IV Part 1
Henry IV Part 2
Henry V
House Made of Dawn
The House of the
    Seven Gables
Huckleberry Finn
I Know Why the
    Caged Bird Sings
Ibsen's Plays I
Ibsen's Plays II
The Idiot
Idylls of the King
The Iliad
Incidents in the Life of
    a Slave Girl
Inherit the Wind
Invisible Man
Ivanhoe
Jane Eyre
Joseph Andrews
The Joy Luck Club
Jude the Obscure

Julius Caesar
The Jungle
Kafka's Short Stories
Keats & Shelley
The Killer Angels
King Lear
The Kitchen God's Wife
The Last of the
    Mohicans
Le Morte d'Arthur
Leaves of Grass
Les Miserables
A Lesson Before Dying
Light in August
The Light in the Forest
Lord Jim
Lord of the Flies
The Lord of the Rings
Lost Horizon
Lysistrata & Other
    Comedies
Macbeth
Madame Bovary
Main Street
The Mayor of
    Casterbridge
Measure for Measure
The Merchant
    of Venice
Middlemarch
A Midsummer Night's
    Dream
The Mill on the Floss
Moby-Dick
Moll Flanders
Mrs. Dalloway
Much Ado About
    Nothing
My Ántonia
Mythology
Narr. …Frederick
    Douglass
Native Son
New Testament
Night
1984
Notes from the
    Underground

Check Out the All-New CliffsNotes Guides

TECHNOLOGY TOPICS

PERSONAL FINANCE TOPICS

CAREER TOPICS